GODS GORILLA GLUE FOR THE CHURCH

ACHIEVING UNITY AMIDST CULTURAL DISCONNECT

Dr. Ralph Swearngin, Jr.

New Harbor Press
RAPID CITY, SD

Copyright © 2023 Ralph Swearngin.

All rights reserved. No part of this publication may be reproduced, distributed or transmitted in any form or by any means, including photocopying, recording, or other electronic or mechanical methods, without the prior written permission of the publisher, except in the case of brief quotations embodied in critical reviews and certain other noncommercial uses permitted by copyright law. For permission requests, write to the publisher, addressed "Attention: Permissions Coordinator," at the address below.

Swearngin/New Harbor Press
1601 Mt. Rushmore Rd, Ste 3288
Rapid City, SD 57701
www.NewHarborPress.com

Ordering Information:
Quantity sales. Special discounts are available on quantity purchases by corporations, associations, and others. For details, contact the "Special Sales Department" at the address above.

God's Gorilla Glue for the Church / Ralph Swearngin. —1st ed.
ISBN 978-1-63357-438-0

CONTENTS

I. INTRODUCTION AND BASIC ASSUMPTIONS 1

II. FRACTURES IN THE NEW TESTAMENT CHURCH 17

III. PRESCRIPTIONS FOR UNITY IN THE NEW
   TESTAMENT CHURCH 35

IV. THE CONTEMPORARY CHURCH AND CULTURE 49

V. UNDERSTANDING CULTURAL CHANGE
   IN THE CONTEMPORARY CHURCH 65

VI. CULTURAL DISCONNECT IN THE
   EXPECTATIONS OF THE CHURCH 73

VII. CULTURAL DISCONNECT IN THE
   METHODS OF THE CHURCH 89

VIII. CULTURAL DISCONNECT IN
   PROCLAIMING THE MESSAGE OF THE CHURCH 97

IX. PRINCIPLES FOR UNITING A
   CHANGING CHURCH 105

I

INTRODUCTION AND BASIC ASSUMPTIONS

MY GOAL FOR READERS of this book is that they understand the importance of unity among followers of Christ at a time when there are cultural influences that keep many believers separated from one another. In order to get to some principles for reaching unity in the church today, you will take a quick trip back to the first century to see how the Early Church was able to find unity when fractures occurred in the Body of Christ. In order to bridge the time span from the first century to the twenty-first century, you will venture into some social and communication theories that explain both cultural disconnect and pathways to unity. Finally, we will get to a practical analysis of cultural factors that disconnect believers today, and some principles for unifying those believers to fulfill God's mission for the church.

God wants disconnected Christians to be united in order to fulfill His plans for the church. When many of us think about putting things back together, we think about Gorilla Glue. According to Wikipedia, Mark Singer marketed a polyurethane adhesive in 1994 and named it *Gorilla Glue*. Later, the line of products produced by the Gorilla Glue Company expanded to include tapes, epoxies, and other such adhesives. Most of their advertising depicts people breaking something and realizing they need to repair it. At that point, they are pleasantly surprised when a gorilla appears and gives them some Gorilla Glue to fix the broken object.

God has plans to unite disconnected believers that are far more effective than Gorilla Glue. In this book, I have tried to identify some of the causes for cultural disconnect in churches, and to demonstrate how God can bring about unity in the Body of Christ.

One of the greatest challenges facing the contemporary church involves securing and maintaining unity in the white-water rapids of cultural change. I am amazed at videos I have seen with people navigating perilous rapids in rafts. The rafts get turned in all directions—even upside down. Rapid social change has a similar effect on institutions in our society, and the church is one of those institutions. The issues addressed in this book are ones that often provoke feelings of discomfort and discontent in Christians, but those issues must be confronted because they divide and diminish the effectiveness of local congregations. If you are aware of feeling uncomfortable and disconnected from other believers in regard to your experiences with the church, you may not understand the sources of those feelings. Perhaps, by identifying and understanding the challenges to unity in the church, you will be able to handle those challenges (and your feelings) more effectively. When believers are disconnected by cultural differences, it can create fractures in the Body of Christ, the church.

In this book I will use two different words to describe disunity among followers of Christ. When I am referring to disunity in the structure of the church, I will refer to it as *fractures in the Body of Christ*. When I am referring to disunity among believers (individually or corporately), I will refer to it as *disconnect*.

A television commercial in the past used the slogan, "It's not your father's Oldsmobile." That signified that something new and different was being produced by this longtime automobile manufacturer. I realize that some people reading this book might not even know there was such a brand of automobile, since they are no longer being made. The push for things that are new and different is still evident in nearly every area of American life. For many people, "it's not your father's church" is an observation that brings emotional discomfort. As the twenty-first century unfolds, it is apparent that Christians need to determine what precepts and practices in the church should be maintained, and what things can be changed to adapt to the culture in which it operates and still remain within the parameters of God's will. When the distinctions between God's messages and human methods get blurred, there can be a tendency to rely on what is familiar and comfortable in our personal experiences. When believers make the usage of familiar methodology a test of fellowship for other believers, they are remaking the church into their design instead of following God's design. Spiritual growth involves digging into the messages from God's Word that bring new insights to us, and that can be somewhat discomforting.

In all likelihood, there has never been a time of more widespread diversity in American culture than the twenty-first century. So much attention has been given to the term *diversity* that it seems to be a buzzword people use without having a full understanding of its implications. Census data confirms that diverse groups of people live in America, but that does not reveal the full picture of what is happening in this nation. A more useful concept to aid our understanding of contemporary American culture is "pluralism." According to the Merriam–Webster dictionary, *pluralism* is the "state of living in which members of diverse ethnic, racial, religious, or social groups maintain and develop their traditional culture within a common society." That definition is lacking one important category of people who are referenced in this book. In addition to the categories listed above, there are people who have lived in different eras of social change. Those differences are important considerations in any discussion of pluralism.

Diana Eck created the Pluralism Project at Harvard University to study growing religious diversity in the United States. In her writings viewed on the website of the Pluralism Project (pluralism.org), Eck formulated some helpful insights about a pluralistic society. Eck stressed that pluralism is more than diversity, because pluralism involves developing relationships among diverse people even in the face of cultural tension. The mere presence of diverse people in one location does not guarantee that those people will want to or be able to work together. Pluralistic relationships will only thrive when there is honest dialogue (both talking and listening) that leads to a better understanding of each other's background and experiences. Eck stressed that pluralism does not require diverse people to relinquish the cultural backgrounds that make them different from others. In a pluralistic paradigm, there is likelihood that different points of view will remain when diverse people interact with each other harmoniously.

For many generations, American culture was described as a "melting pot" in which immigrants relinquished their cultural heritage in order to form one homogeneous American culture. The theory of the melting pot was that everyone would end up speaking and acting alike in order to live in a monolithic American culture. The pluralistic paradigm suggests that diverse groups of people can live and work together while maintaining some of their cultural roots, even though there might be varying degrees of tension as people learn to work through their differences. There is some evidence that the ideological clash between the one-culture advocates and the advocates of pluralism is a social issue that divides this nation today. A basic assumption in this book is that America is a pluralistic society, and learning to live in that environment is creating a number of challenges for local congregations.

Here is an illustration of pluralism at work in an area in which I have had some experience. For nearly twenty-five years, I officiated high school football games. For more than twenty-two years after that, I trained officials in a number of sports. Let's say that a football crew is comprised of two Caucasian officials, two African–American officials, and one Latino official. Two of those officials are business professionals, two are construction workers, and one is a student. Three of the officials are older than forty-five years of age and the other two are younger than forty-five. That crew would be considered to have diverse cultural backgrounds. When they officiate in a game, they work together to accomplish the mission of enforcing rules to keep the game under control while not forfeiting their cultural identities. I believe this illustration can be applied to a discussion about unity in the church in the midst of a variety of cultural influences.

Many discussions on topics such as diversity, pluralism, or unity place their focus on race, ethnicity, and gender. Those are valid categories to study, but generational differences in America need to be added to our discussions. The rapid speed of social change creates cultural chasms between generations of people.

Another basic assumption in this book is that there is value in knowing what the Bible has to say about the relationship between cultural issues and following Christ—specifically, in matters involving the mission of the church. The diversity inherent in a pluralistic society can fragment Christians into camps of differing opinions and practices. If Christians want to know how to develop unity in local congregations today, there is value in knowing how the early Christians developed unity in the church as they overcame divisions that arose due to cultural differences. However, it is important to realize that a study of the church described in the New Testament must involve understanding what issues are valid for the church in all cultures and for all eras, and what issues arose because of specific cultural influences found in the first century. A major difference in today's church and the New Testament church is the factor of extremely rapid social change and its impact on our thoughts and attitudes. That increased speed of social change is an important issue that will be examined in this book.

In most instances in this book, the term *church* will refer to the universal Body of Christ. When the term is applied to a local congregation or a group of congregations, I will try to specify that. A logical starting point for how Christians should carry out the mission of the church is to look at God's ideal plan for the church as revealed in Scripture. Throughout the Bible, human sinfulness circumvented God's ideal plans for His kingdom. The disruptions in God's plans for the church can be seen in the fractures that occurred in the New Testament church. Since God is eternally sovereign as well as full of mercy, He cares about His wandering people and He has a plan to bring them back to Him. The fragmentation found in the Early Church led the Holy Spirit to direct New Testament writers to extend pleas for unity in the church to heal those fractures. Understanding both the source of the fractures in the Early Church and the prescribed paths to restore unity can provide important insights for us today. That process of fragmentation and restoration of unity is still evident in the life of local congregations that are in the midst of pluralism and rapid social change.

The first two chapters of Genesis describe God's ideal creation of the world that began with a man and a woman being placed in a perfect environment. God only had one prohibition in the Garden of Eden. Adam and Eve were not to eat the fruit of the tree of the knowledge of good and evil. The free will that God created in Adam and Eve allowed them to exercise choices that disobeyed God's command. Their disobedience created a separation between God and themselves, and it changed God's perfect creation into a world that began a process of ongoing deterioration. God created humans with the intent to relate to them, so the separation between the Creator and His creation needed to be repaired.

God designed several approaches to bring people back into a relationship with Him, and He had a timetable for fulfilling this task. God dealt directly with the patriarchs like Abraham, Isaac, Jacob, and even Joseph. God established *covenants* (bilateral agreements) with those people in which He promised care and blessings, and He demanded their obedience. God was constant with His blessings, but the people were not steadfast in their obedience. Therefore, God unveiled the next step for reconciliation in which He gave Moses a set of laws to show the Israelites what God desired them to obey. The law provided a mirror for the Israelites to see where they were transgressing God's commands.

Because laws don't make people behave appropriately all the time, God went to the next step in His process. God provided human messengers, the prophets, to remind the people of God's care, His commands, and His punishments for disobedience. God's intent for the prophets was to redirect people's lives from disobedience to obedience. God revealed through these messengers that He could not coexist with sinfulness, and there would be punishment for disobedience. Prophets also reminded people of God's constant love and care even when troubles occurred in their lives as individuals or as a nation. The prophets also told people about God's provisions for ultimate victories in the future through the Messiah.

People didn't always respond favorably toward the prophets, and God moved to His ultimate plan as recorded in **Galatians 4:4–5 [NIV]**.

> *But when the right time had fully come, God sent His Son, born of a woman, born under the law to redeem those under the law that we might receive the full rights of sons.*

When Christ came to earth in human form, He brought God's New Covenant to all the world. Christ came to earth to live a *godly lifestyle* (without sin), to teach people about God's eternal kingdom, and to die on a cross to redeem humanity from sin. Then, after God resurrected Christ from the dead to secure eternal victory over death, Christ returned to the Father.

The cross of Christ did not end God's plan to maintain a love relationship with His people. The ministry of reconciliation that Christ had begun needed to be continued. Under the direction of the Holy Spirit, the church was established to continue Jesus' ministry here on earth. The church was established by God to carry on the ministry of Christ to bring people into His Kingdom, to nurture their spiritual growth in a world that did not support such growth, and to provide care and encouragement for believers until Christ returned to earth. This was a well-thought-out plan that had several processes imbedded in it. The components of God's plan (the Law, Prophets, Christ, and Church) were not "Plan B, C, D" provisions. God decided on the complete plan before creation, and each step of His plan was implemented at the time and in the way He desired. The apostle Paul taught that to the Ephesian believers as we find in **Ephesians 1:4 [NLT]**:

> **Even before He made the world, God loved us and chose us in Christ to be holy and without fault in His eyes. God decided in advance to adopt us into His own family by bringing us to Himself through Jesus Christ.**

The New Testament reveals God's plans for the church, and His model for the church should be our focal point as we look to discover ways for the church to be most effective in the twenty-first century. One part of God's plan for the church involves the ministry of reconciliation that Paul described in **II Corinthians 5:17–19 [NIV]**:

> *Therefore, if any one is in Christ, he is a new creation; the old has gone, the new has come! All this is from God, who reconciled us to Himself through Christ and gave us the ministry of reconciliation; that God was reconciling the world to Himself in Christ, not counting men's sins against them. And He committed to us the message of reconciliation.*

God designed that ministry to draw people back to Him when we find ourselves digressing from what He wants His church to be. Reconciliation is foundational to unity in the church. Believers who are reconciled to God are expected to be united with each other spiritually.

References to the church in the New Testament use the Greek word *ekklesia*, which is defined as a "duly convened assembly of citizens." According to William Barclay (*New Testament Words*), this concept was understood by people from Greek, Hebrew, and Roman cultures. In the Greek translation of the Old Testament, *ekklesia* is used seventy times to indicate situations in which God called together His people so they could listen to Him or act for Him. The church is an intentional design by God to achieve His goals for His Kingdom, and that design is still relevant today. As sociologists and anthropologists developed their studies of cultures worldwide, the church became labeled a social institution. In that kind of conceptual framework, the church has been viewed as something that was created by humans to enhance their cultures. That is not accurate.

God sets the parameters for who can be a part of the "called together" by ordaining the process of how a person is adopted into His family. This differentiates the church from a club or other kind of organization in which members make rules about who is allowed into the group and sets the procedures for how the group operates. The New Testament delineates the essential parameters for constituting the church.

God created the church to be an action-based entity, and not a passive group of believers. God expects the church to be functional in carrying out the ministry that Christ left for His followers. God has always intended for the church to be a vital, working part of His Kingdom. God designed His Kingdom to grow and develop through the work of the *"ekklesia"* that is directed by the Holy Spirit. That work begins with evangelism as was seen in the events on the Day of Pentecost as described in **Acts 2:41–42 [NIV]**.

> *Those who accepted the message were baptized, and about 3,000 were added to their number that day. They devoted themselves to the apostles' teaching, and to the fellowship, to the breaking of bread, and to prayer.*

It is important to note in this passage that some things occurred before the people were added to the church, and some things occurred after they were added. Before they were added to the church, the people listened to the Good News that Peter preached, they repented, and they were baptized. There is no indication that being added to the church involved any paperwork to be completed or any vote to be taken about accepting them as members. Those people believed the gospel message and accepted Christ as their Savior and Lord and were baptized.

After they had been added to the church, the believers devoted themselves to spiritual growth, to fellowship, and to prayer. Evangelism is not the only mission of the church, but it is an essential aspect of the mission. Jesus' commission for His apostles (and all subsequent followers of Christ) is to "make disciples" throughout the world (**Matthew 28:19–20**). Disciples are made through a process of conversion, baptism, and teaching them to obey Jesus' commands.

Jesus told Nicodemus that becoming a follower of His involved a spiritual rebirth. Spiritual rebirth has some parallels to physical birth procedures. For example, after a baby is born, the parents don't consider the process to be completed. They don't leave the baby in the hospital nursery; but rather, they take the baby home to complete the process of nurture and development. After evangelism has productive results, the new Christians must be nurtured in order to grow spiritually. Both evangelism and nurture are important responsibilities in the contemporary church. The process of nurture often involves uniting disconnected believers.

The mission of the church also involves equipping the believers as Paul taught the church at Ephesus in **Ephesians 4:11–13 [NIV]**.

> *It was He (Christ) who gave some to be apostles, some to be prophets, some to be evangelists, and some to be pastors and teachers to prepare God's people for works of service so that the body of Christ may be built up until we all reach unity in the faith and in the knowledge of the Son of God and to become mature, attaining to the whole measure of the fullness of Christ.*

The word in the Greek that is translated as *equip* was used in several contexts in the first century. In the field of medicine, that word was used for setting a broken bone. For fishermen, that term was used to describe mending torn nets. In government and politics, the word was used for bringing together opposing factions to complete a task. The basic intent for equipping involves putting things or persons into a condition that enables them to function effectively.

Equipping saints is a lifelong restoration process for every believer that is best facilitated in the church. As we will discuss in depth later in this book, there are times when relationships in the church are fractured, and those disjointed body parts need to be set for proper healing. There are times when the torn nets in the relationships of believers need to be mended. And there are times when opposing factions need to be brought together in unity so the work of the church can be carried out effectively.

As was noted earlier, the church needs to nurture people as they grow spiritually. Paul emphasized this point in **Colossians 1:9–12a [NIV]**.

> **For this reason, since the day we heard about you, we have not stopped praying for you and asking God to fill you with the knowledge of His will through all spiritual wisdom and understanding. And we pray this in order that you may live a life worthy of the Lord and may please Him in every way: bearing fruit in every good work, growing in the knowledge of God, being strengthened with all power according to His glorious might so that you may have great endurance and patience, and joyfully giving thanks to the Father....**

Paul gave the Colossians a process for spiritual growth that begins with knowing God's will through spiritual wisdom and understanding. God is a God of revelation, so He communicates His will through His word. The idea that we need to search for God's will like it is a "spiritual needle in a haystack" is not a New Testament concept. The indwelling Holy Spirit provides spiritual wisdom and understanding as we study God's Word, and as we commune with God in prayer. That process of enhanced spiritual knowledge enables a believer to live a productive life that honors God and pleases Him. Paul indicated that the goal of spiritual growth is to know God better and better. That is a cycle in which increased knowledge of God produces increased spiritual growth and productivity, and we get to know God even better in the process.

Spiritual growth is something that each individual Christian experiences to enhance his or her relationship with God, but that growth also enhances his or her relationships with other believers. That is a very meaningful aspect of God's plans for the church. God intended for individual believers to interact with each other in order to form a cohesive network of growing Christians who know God better and better. When the relationships among believers are strained or broken, the church loses its focus and its effectiveness.

One of the most vivid word pictures in the New Testament describes the church as the Body of Christ. This is where physiology meets theology. Physiology is the branch of biology that deals with the normal functioning of living organisms and their parts. The description of a spiritually based organism that is expressed in terms of a physical human body, paints a vivid picture of God's design—both for human bodies and for the church. Let's look at several passages in the New Testament that describe the importance of connectivity in the functioning of the Body of Christ, the church.

> **Ephesians 1:22–23 [NIV]**
> **And God placed all things under His (Christ's) feet and appointed Him to be head over everything for the church, which is His body, the fullness of Him who fills everything in every way.**
>
> **Ephesians 4:15–16 [NIV]**
> **Instead, speaking the truth in love, we will in all things grow up into Him who is the Head, that is, Christ. From Him the whole body, joined and held together by every supporting ligament, grows and builds itself up in love, as each part does its work.**

Let's apply what we know about physiology to God's language about the church. The brain controls body functioning unless artificial medical procedures are used to sustain some technical form of life. Each body part (organ, bone, joint, or connective tissue) fulfills a distinct function for the body to perform properly and effectively. Those body parts have different types of composition, and are designed for different purposes. Those diverse body parts have to be coordinated in order for the body to be healthy and functional, and that is the responsibility of the brain.

James Weldon Johnson wrote the song "Dry Bones" that was first recorded by the Famous Myers Jubilee Singers in 1928. This song was inspired by the prophetic writings in **Ezekiel 37** about dry bones being reconnected. The song vividly depicts the importance of having the various bones in the body connected to one another properly.

Toe bone connected to the foot bone
Foot bone connected to the heel bone
Heel bone connected to the ankle bone
Ankle bone connected to the shin bone
Shin bone connected to the knee bone
Knee bone connected to the thigh bone
Thigh bone connected to the hip bone
Hip bone connected to the back bone
Back bone connected to the shoulder bone
Shoulder bone connected to the neck bone
Neck bone connected to the head bone
Now hear the word of the Lord.

That connectivity in the human body is carried out by *ligaments* (connective tissue that attaches bone to bone) and *tendons* (connective tissue that enables movement of the bones by connecting them to muscle). When all the body parts are connected properly to each other, and when the head (brain) is working properly, the human body is a magnificent creation capable of many wonderful things.

However, when one or more body parts stop functioning as needed, other body parts try to compensate for the deficiency. That compensation process usually results in further physical damage. For example, have you ever sprained an ankle or knee and still tried to walk around. Not only does this slow down the healing process in the injured body part, but it is also likely to produce harm to your hip or back. Just like the human body, the church functions best when all the parts of the body are working together under the guidance of its "head"—Jesus Christ. When the members of Christ's Body are not properly united, the whole body is less effective. It is important to remember that God's plans are not stymied by human impediments. However, those divisions render Christians (individually and corporately) less effective than they could be. Our all-knowing, all-powerful God knows how to work around divisions in the church so His Kingdom can prevail, but God's original plan is based on the unity of His people.

Now that my foundational assumptions have been revealed, let's take a deeper dive into the study of how God has planted His *outposts* (local congregations) in a world whose cultures divide people in a number of ways.

II

FRACTURES IN THE NEW TESTAMENT CHURCH

DESPITE GOD'S PLAN FOR the church, a variety of issues have plagued the church throughout history as Satan attempts to thwart God's plans. Scripture indicates that Christ won the war against Satan on the cross, but Satan still conducts skirmishes to try to impede the progress of the church. Those skirmishes don't change the outcome for the church, but they can take a toll on individuals in the church.

Skirmishes that didn't affect the outcome of a war have been seen in American history.

One example occurred at the second attack on Fort Bowyer, which was located at the mouth of Mobile Bay in Alabama. On February 8, 1815, the British fleet began to attack the fort. The battle raged for three days until the British surrendered on February 11th. During that battle, the British casualties amounted to thirteen dead and eighteen wounded, while the American casualties were recorded as one dead and ten wounded. On February 13, 1815, word got to Fort Bowyer that the Treaty of Ghent had been signed in December of 1814. The war had officially ended two months prior to this battle.

The Battle of Fort Bowyer didn't change the outcome of the war, but it affected the lives of a number of people.

In a somewhat more recent example, we might look at the exploits of Hiroo Onoda. Onoda was a Japanese army officer in World War II assigned to defend the island of Lubang in the Philippines in 1944. As America gained control of the islands in the Pacific, Onoda found himself in command of just three other soldiers. On September 2, 1945, the treaty was signed that officially ended the war with Japan, but for the next twenty-nine years, Onoda carried out guerrilla warfare in the jungle of Lubang in the belief that he was fulfilling the assignment given to him in 1944.

It is estimated that Onoda and his crew killed thirty people and wounded over one hundred people long after the war was officially over. The US and Philippine governments even dropped leaflets throughout the jungle announcing the signing of the treaty to end the war, but Onoda thought it was a ruse to get him to surrender. A Japanese student researching Onoda trekked through the jungle and found him, but Onoda refused to believe this student and said he would only stop fighting when his commanding officer told him to do so. The governments of Japan, the Philippines, and the United States arranged for the officer who ordered Onoda to Lubang (who was working in a bookstore in Japan) to go to Onoda. Only then did Onoda surrender his sword (in full dress uniform) to President Marcos of the Philippines.

Satan's skirmishes against and within the church are evident throughout the New Testament epistles. Using the metaphor of the church as the Body of Christ, the New Testament describes a number of fractures in the Body, and those fractures are present in local congregations today. By understanding the source of the fractures in the New Testament churches, we might be able to recognize issues that keep the Body of Christ from functioning properly today.

I don't believe the writers of the New Testament epistles delivered hypothetical messages to the churches. When they wrote, they addressed real issues in the lives of the people and in the operation of the churches to whom they wrote. When the writers warned about issues that were harming the Body of Christ, those issues must have been an actual part of the lives of the readers. When they wrote about the need for unity in a New Testament church, there must have been some type of disunity in that situation.

It is detrimental to the health of the church (universally and locally) when fractures occur, just like fractures in our physical bodies are detrimental to our health. Regardless of the root causes of the fracture, there are several harmful results that occur and believers are disconnected from one another. The people in a fractured local congregation often tend to exhibit exclusionary behaviors that create and maintain separation from other people. In many instances, multiple factions develop as each group stakes out its territory (theologically, culturally, or in some other way). Group pride tends to grow within each faction in the church, and that erodes unity among the believers even further. In this situation, people promote a deliberate disconnection from those who don't agree with them.

The apostle Paul addressed the need for the church to be inclusive and connected when he wrote to the believers in the church at Corinth in **I Corinthians 12:13 [NIV]**:

> **The body is a unit though it is made up of many parts; and though all its parts are many, they form one body. So it is with Christ. For we were all baptized by one Spirit into one body—whether Jews or Greeks, slave or free—and we were all given the one Spirit to drink.**

When there are fractures in a local congregation, that church stagnates and its influence shrinks, just like muscles in the body atrophy when a fractured limb is placed in a cast to prevent movement. And, if the fractures in the church aren't healed, full-scale division is likely to occur in that congregation. The fractures found in the New Testament church were caused by a number of issues, and I have selected several causes for study that seem to have occurred with some frequency.

Fractures from Ungodly Thinking

Jude, a half-brother of Jesus, wrote his epistle in order to expose false teachers who were leading Christians away from the teachings of Jesus. His writing also was intended to encourage believers as they grew their faith. We find one issue that Jude identified as creating fractures in the church in **Jude 17–19 [NIV]**:

> **But, dear friends, remember what the apostles of our Lord Jesus Christ foretold. They said to you, "In the last times there will be scoffers who will follow their own ungodly desires." These are the men who divide you, who follow mere natural instincts and do not have the Spirit.**

At first glance, we might think that "scoffers of God" would be nonbelievers. But, if that were the case here, there would not be divisions in the church. These scoffers were a part of the church. The people that Jude blamed for creating fractures in the church scoffed at spiritual things, and were devoted to satisfying their ungodly desires. The Greek word for *scoff* paints a word picture of someone who rejects something with vigorous contempt. The scoffers were inflicting real damage among the believers, and Jude described that damage as a division in the body. The word translated *divide* here is a Greek word that refers to attitudes more than overt actions. This is a deeper kind of division because attitudes are often hidden. Those attitudes can permeate every aspect of the work of the church without people being aware. In many areas of life, we encounter the mistaken assumption that just getting people to stop certain actions will change them. Behavior will be modified long-term when thoughts and attitudes are changed; then, actions will change.

Jude believed that the Body of Christ was fractured due to carnal thinking instead of spiritual thinking, and that carnal thinking was leading people away from Christ and His Good News. Since the head of the church is Christ, members of the body whose attitudes are not spiritually motivated cannot function in the church as God intended—these body parts want to have a mind of their own instead of the mind of Christ.

Paul also wrote to believers about people whose attitudes and actions did not reflect God's intentions for the church when they met together in **I Corinthians 11:17–18 [NIV]**.

> **In the following directives I have no praise for you, for your meetings do more harm than good. In the first place, I hear that when you come together as a church, there are divisions among you, and to some extent I believe it.**

Paul based his concerns on reports he had gotten about the way the Corinthians acted when they came together to eat. The sharing of meals by Christians that was mentioned in **Acts 2:46** became a significant experience among other Christians as the church grew. The practice mentioned in this text is often referred to as a "love feast." It was much like a carry-in dinner in today's church, except that, in the early days of the church, the Lord's Supper (the ordinance of communion) was incorporated in this event.

Paul had received a report that fellowship in the church had been hurt by the actions of some of the people who were creating divisions. The people that Paul accused of not being interested in the Lord's Supper demonstrated their ungodly thinking by rejecting the very reason for the church to meet together. Paul indicated that there will be differences in a local congregation when some people obey God (receiving God's approval) and others do not, but those differences need to be addressed and resolved so that the Body of Christ doesn't become fractured.

Fractures Due to Cross-Cultural Issues

The church was not very old as a movement when internal dissension arose between two different groups of Jewish believers living in Jerusalem. There were Jews from Palestine who considered themselves pure Jews. There were also Jews from other regions who had been saved on the Day of Pentecost, and they came from cultures where Greek was spoken. While both groups of Jews were aligned in their antagonism toward Gentiles, Luke records an incident in which there was dissension among Jewish believers themselves in **Acts 6:1–4 [NIV]**.

> **In those days when the number of disciples was increasing, the Grecian Jews among them complained against the Hebraic Jews because their widows were being overlooked in the daily distribution of food. So the Twelve gathered all the disciples together and said, "It would not be right for us to neglect the ministry of the word of God in order to wait on tables. Brothers, choose seven men from among you who are known to be full of the Spirit and wisdom. We will turn the responsibility over to them and we will give our attention to prayer and the ministry of the word."**

This fracture in the church in Jerusalem arose over the care of the widows. The Hellenistic Jews complained that their widows were treated unfairly by the local Jews when it came to the daily distribution of food to those in need. That daily distribution was a long-standing Jewish practice that the Early Church continued. The leaders in the church in Jerusalem wisely decided to set up a structure of care that would meet the needs of the widows without taking away from the teaching of the Good News that was enlarging the Body of Christ. The cultural differences seen within the church in Jerusalem can still be seen in churches today. There are degrees of diversity within every racial or ethnic group. Even when attendees are from the same racial or ethnic group, there are people who have diverse geographic and/or educational backgrounds. And that does not even address personality differences that occur when people interact.

When the first-century church began evangelizing Gentiles, the interaction of Jews and Gentiles in the church did not go harmoniously all the time. For a variety of reasons, both doctrinal and cultural differences contributed to fractures in the church. The apostle Paul had taken the lead in evangelizing Gentiles, and the Holy Spirit was evident in that work. Paul's ministry was not accepted by some of the other apostles, and he told the church at Galatia about a divisive episode that involved cultural differences in **Galatians 2:11–13 [NIV]**:

> **When Peter came to Antioch, I opposed him to his face because he was clearly in the wrong. Before certain men came from James, he used to eat with Gentiles. But when they arrived, he began to draw back and separate himself from the Gentiles because he was afraid of those who belonged to the circumcision group. The other Jews joined him in his hypocrisy so that by their hypocrisy even Barnabas was led astray.**

Some readers might think that the root of this issue was really a doctrinal issue (whether Christians needed to be circumcised in accordance with traditional Jewish law), but I want to focus the interpersonal dynamics of this situation and its impact on the fellowship among believers. The fabric of the fellowship of the church at Antioch had to be damaged by Peter's hypocrisy. *Hypocrisy* is often defined as being two-faced, and that describes Peter's behavior. It reminds me of some of the issues we faced in high school about wanting to eat with the "cool people" and leaving out some others. Jewish culture had taboos about a Jew eating with a Gentile, but Peter disregarded that until strong cultural pressures led him to revert back to behaviors from his past.

Paul challenged Peter for his weakness of wanting to avoid criticism from the folks in the "mother church" in Jerusalem. Peter wasn't alone in this hypocrisy, but his behavior was high profile and caught the attention of other believers. What intrigues me is that this situation arose after Peter's traditional Jewish beliefs had been challenged by God in a vision in Joppa. After God got his attention, Peter had preached to Cornelius (a Gentile), and Cornelius' conversion resulted in the Holy Spirit being poured out on Gentiles. Peter was cognitively aware of God's work with Gentiles, but cultural influences and his ego overrode his thinking processes. Trying to live up to the expectations of others can sometimes divert a person from doing what he or she knows to be right, and it can create fractures in the Body of Christ.

Fractures Due to Doctrinal Issues

Since there were no printed copies of the New Testament in the first century, the Early Church relied on letters from apostles like Paul and on the spoken word of traveling preachers and teachers. These diverse messengers of religious thought did not always teach the authentic Good News that the apostles taught. When the new Christians relied on a variety of people sharing oral teachings, false teachers prevailed and fractures developed in the church.

The gospel of Christ varied greatly from the teaching of Judaism and the philosophies of Greece. Accepting the gospel required first-century believers to put aside a number of preexisting beliefs, and that presented some challenges. A number of the traveling preachers tried to blend Christianity into the Greek philosophies they had believed before becoming a Christian. That was evident in the way that Gnosticism infiltrated the Early Church. Additionally, some Jewish teachers wanted to hold onto as much of their Jewish religious heritage as possible, and that was the fuel that fed the work of the Judaizers.

As the Early Church spread from Jerusalem to other parts of the world, believers still looked to the leaders in the church at Jerusalem for ultimate answers to their doctrinal questions. Paul was an apostle who was called directly by Christ to spread the gospel, so he was quite capable of teaching people the authentic Good News. Paul's adversaries, however, challenged his authority and his teachings, and that created doubts in the minds of people in many of the embryonic congregations. The Judaizers spread a doctrine that required Gentile believers to follow traditional Jewish teachings with Jesus' teachings tacked on at the end. Paul taught that Jewish customs were not a part of becoming a follower of Christ. Therefore, those confused people in the church at Antioch wanted to receive clarification from the leaders in the "mother church" in Jerusalem in order to resolve the doctrinal debates. An important description of this divisive issue is found in **Acts 15:1–2 [NIV]**.

> **Some men came down from Judea to Antioch and were teaching the brothers: "Unless you are circumcised according to the custom taught by Moses, you cannot be saved." This brought Paul and Barnabas into sharp dispute and debate with them. So Paul and Barnabas were appointed, along with some**

> **other believers, to go up to Jerusalem to see the apostles and elders about this question.**

Paul and Barnabas were sent to discuss the doctrinal issues raised in Antioch with the elders in Jerusalem. There was a need to resolve the disputes that had arisen when Judaizers tried to contradict the doctrines that Paul taught. Discussions at this meeting of the Council revealed that fractures over the same doctrinal issues that existed in Antioch also existed in the church in Jerusalem.

Think about the church back at Antioch while all this turmoil was going on. How could that group of believers move forward in their spiritual growth if they weren't sure about what they were supposed to believe? Was circumcision essential for salvation or not? But this issue was wider in scope than just the church at Antioch. The Early Church was being divided by groups whose teachings were being debated. God did empower the first-century churches to prevail over the false teachings, but the cost of time and effort in working through the fractures was significant for many people. That is an important truth to consider. God will see that His Kingdom prevails despite the challenges that arise in local congregations.

There are at least two aspects of those doctrinal disputes that need to be considered—beliefs and behavior. Beliefs involve a body of facts about the gospel plus the faith to move beyond the facts to accept spiritual things. The behavioral aspects address how people relate to one another as they deal with doctrinal differences. Paul was concerned about both aspects, because both had a direct effect on the unity of the church. It isn't just what you believe that is important. How you say what you believe has to be consistent with the attitudes of Christ, the head of the church. Have you ever been in a situation where someone speaks things you agree with, but the way they express their thoughts makes you wish you didn't agree with them? The Body of Christ can be fractured by doctrinally correct people who alienate others with their actions and attitudes.

Paul mentored Timothy on how to be a servant leader in churches that did not always agree on their doctrinal beliefs, and didn't always "play well" with each other. He addressed that issue in **II Timothy 2:14–16 [NIV]**.

> **Keep reminding them of these things. Warn them before God against quarreling about words; it is of no value, and only ruins those who listen. Do your best to present yourself to God as one approved, a workman who does not need to be ashamed and who correctly handles the word of truth. Avoid godless chatter, because those who indulge in it will become more and more ungodly.**

At the time Paul wrote this letter to Timothy, the roots of the heresy of Gnosticism were developing, and that fractured unity in many churches. Advocates of this heresy tried to twist the simple gospel and turn it into a complex Greek philosophy. The Greeks really liked to debate ideas as Paul found out when they met with Greek philosophers on Mars Hill in Athens (**Acts 17:16–34**). Those false teachers thought it was important to parse words in order to stimulate debate. The presence of these debates opened the door to arguments by other people who wanted to explore new ideas in order to take the gospel in different directions. Therefore, fractures developed in the Body of Christ as diverse doctrinal debates raged.

The gospel injected new ideas into the minds of Jews, Greeks, and Romans. There are several ways that people can manage conflicting ideas. The concept of assimilation suggests that new ideas are disregarded or modified in some way to fit into what a person already believes. The concept of accommodation suggests that existing beliefs are adjusted to accept new ideas. That was the process that people from Jewish, Greek, and Roman cultural backgrounds had to go through when they received the gospel. Many of the hearers accepted the Good News of Jesus Christ fully, and that replaced their previous thoughts and actions. Others rejected the gospel immediately because it didn't fit with their existing mindset. These people were often the ones most adamant in their persecution of Christians. There were some people (like the Judaizers and the Gnostics) who tried to merge the new ideas about Christ with their previous beliefs and practices. Jesus addressed the futility of this approach in **Luke 5:36 [NIV]**.

> **He told them this parable: "No one tears a patch from a new garment and sews it on an old one. If he does, he will have torn the new garment, and the patch from the new will not match the old."**

Paul warned Timothy about the damage that the debates were inflicting on the believers young Timothy was leading, but the principles Paul was expounding can apply to all churches. Paul said these conversations had no value. Paul said that these arguments over the right word to use did not benefit the church. The issue here appears to be that these believers were majoring in minors. They were debating issues that really were not essential to the gospel. Paul also told Timothy that this fighting was ruining the believers involved. The Greek word for *ruining* in this verse, *katastrophe*, is the word used for tearing down a house. This word describes the opposite effect of *edification*, which is a term commonly used in the New Testament for building up believers. Paul was a strong proponent of edification. He believed that members of the Body of Christ needed to be growing spiritually. Paul understood that spiritual growth not only involved what a Christian believed, but also how a Christian acted. He tersely explained this important dynamic to the Corinthians believers in **I Corinthians 8:1b [NIV]**:

> *Knowledge puffs up, but love builds up.*

Debates and arguments over spiritual concepts often keep people from living out the very concepts over which they are arguing. People who spend all their time debating and arguing don't have time to carry out the responsibilities that God gave to the church. If all you are doing is "talking the faith," you probably aren't "walking it." That is why Paul encouraged Timothy to work hard at what he was doing in God's Kingdom. As a leader in the church, Timothy was told to encourage his people to focus on the word of truth—God's Word.

Fractures Due to Socioeconomic Issues
Socioeconomic status (SES) is a complex assessment of a person's social class that is usually expressed in relation to the status of others (upper class, middle class, lower class). SES obviously involves an assessment of wealth, but it goes further. SES takes into account one's social position in the community that is often derived from family status or educational attainment. In many cultures, there is a differentiation between "old money" and "new money," so finances are not the only measure of SES. SES was an issue in the Jewish, Greek, and Roman cultures in the first century since all three cultures had their versions of status assessments that included family heritage, wealth, and whether you were a free person or a slave.

The issues associated with socioeconomic status found their way into the workings of the Early Church. The Book of James may be the most practically focused book in the New Testament. James was outspoken about some of the SES-related problems he had witnessed in the church (probably the church in Jerusalem where he held a leadership position) in **James 2:1–4 [NIV].**

> **My brothers, as believers in our glorious Lord Jesus Christ, don't show favoritism. Suppose a man comes into your meeting wearing a gold ring and fine clothes and a poor man in shabby clothes also comes in. If you show special attention to the man**

> wearing fine clothes and say, "Here's a good seat for you," but say to the poor man, "You stand there" or "Sit on the floor at my feet," have you not discriminated among yourselves and become judges with evil thoughts?

James wrote that a person really can't claim to be a follower of Jesus and still practice favoritism. Playing favorites can be based on many things, but, in this instance, it was based on socioeconomic status. When you favor one person or group over another, you lift up the one and put down the other. This "lift-up and put-down" process obviously fractures relationships, and keeps the church from being the unified Body of Christ. The favoritism that James described is an example of being exclusionary. There were no signs saying, "Poor people can't attend church activities." Both rich and poor were participating in church activities, giving an illusion that the church was open to everyone. According to James, the poor people were made to feel left out, or they were forced to accommodate to the desires of wealthy believers. The favoritism that was shown inflicted wounds (on individuals and to the Body of Christ) when those believers met.

The influence of socioeconomic factors created fractures in other first-century churches. The Early Church contained rich people as well as poor people and slaves, so addressing SES issues straight on was important. Addressing these issues is not as easy as it might seem. Socioeconomic issues are often hidden under what we consider racial or ethnic concerns. Wealthy people may look down on poorer people of their own racial or ethnic group as much as they look down on people of other racial or ethnic groups. Those dynamics were in play in all the cultures in which the Early Church was developing. This is an important consideration in the affluent, pluralistic cultures in which the contemporary church exists.

It would be a mistake to conclude that believers should not possess wealth. The New Testament describes many examples of wealthy people who were generous as they lived out their Christian lives. For example, Paul told Timothy that he had a responsibility as a leader in the church to teach wealthy people how to live as followers of Christ in **I Timothy 6:17–18 [NIV]**.

> **Command those who are rich in this present world not to be arrogant nor to put their hope in wealth, which is so uncertain, but to put their hope in God, who richly provides us with everything for our enjoyment. Command them to do good, to be rich in good deeds, and to be generous and willing to share.**

Paul knew socioeconomic fractures existed in the Early Church, and he urged Timothy to warn rich people how to use their wealth properly. Christians shouldn't be proud that they possess wealth, because Scripture teaches that believers are to be good stewards of all that God provides. Stewards are managers of God's possessions. Good stewards function as conduits in the Body of Christ through which God's blessings are distributed generously to those in need. Paul taught that generosity in this life builds up treasures in heaven, which is what Jesus also taught (**Matthew 19:21**). Paul reminded Timothy that Christians shouldn't trust wealth for real security because real security comes from trusting God. Possessing wealth carries a great responsibility of stewardship. It is a powerful asset when managed properly, but it can be a way to fracture the Body of Christ if misused.

Fractures Due to Personal Preference
The attraction to certain personality types plays an important role in the development of human relationships, and that was true in the first-century church. Some of the early Christians preferred certain individuals to be their leaders, and that sometimes led to fractures within particular congregations. Obviously, some leaders have more

charismatic personalities than others, but that may not be an indication of their spiritual maturity. When the members of the church paid more attention to who was delivering the message than the message itself, problems arose. Even if these leaders were all teaching the authentic gospel, preferences over personalities created fractures in the church. Paul addressed this issue with the Corinthian believers as we find in **I Corinthians 1:11–13 [NIV]**:

> **My brothers, some from Chloe's household have informed me that there are quarrels among you. What I mean is this: One of you says, "I follow Paul"; another, "I follow Apollos"; another, "I follow Cephas"; and still another, "I follow Christ." Is Christ divided? Was Paul crucified for you? Were you baptized in the name of Paul?**

The main issue in this passage involved believers who didn't just have personal preferences about their spiritual leaders; they took pride in "belonging to" that person. The differences in personal preferences led them to quarrel with each other like some of us might argue about which university's football team is the best. Maybe they even had sweatshirts or hats made to advertise their preferences. (*"I belong to Paul," "I belong to Peter," "I belong to Apollos"*) Although each person was entitled to his or her preference about preaching and leadership skills, as Christians, they all needed to realize that they belonged to Christ since they were part of His body! Jealousy and quarreling arose among believers who evidently felt their preferred leader wasn't receiving the respect he was due.

These differences in preferences led to quarrels with enough animosity that Paul called it a full-fledged division in the church. The Greek word used for *division* (*schisma*) was the word used for tearing a garment. These divisions were literally tearing the fabric of the church apart. Paul reminded his readers that dividing into factions was common in the world outside the church, but God's Kingdom demands unity.

Fractures Due to Self-Righteous Attitudes
Learning to accept God's grace graciously was difficult for some believers in the first century, and it remains a difficulty for some people in the twenty-first century. It may be similar to the attitudes of poor winners that we sometimes see in athletics. When human egos get in the way of accepting our place in the Body of Christ, fractures will occur in the church. Paul addressed this issue in **Galatians 5:26** and **6:3–5 [NIV]**.

> **Let us not become conceited, provoking and envying each other . . . If anyone thinks he is something when he is nothing, he deceives himself. Each one should take pride in himself, without comparing himself to somebody else, for each one should carry his own load.**

Some people might use terms like *pride* or *arrogance* instead of *self-righteousness* to describe Paul's focus in this passage. However, in the Early Church, people who displayed self-centeredness in the work of the church often did so because they considered themselves to be more righteous or more spiritual than other people. Those are attitudes that still exist in the contemporary church.

Most people are fairly skilled at selective self-assessments. We know who to compare ourselves to depending on whether we want to look good or look bad in that comparison. Paul told the Galatian believers that they needed to focus on what they were doing for Christ without judging what others were or were not doing. When Christians focus on their perceived spiritual superiority, the only assistance they will give to others tends to be patronizing or condescending. When one part of the body of Christ determines that he or she is more important than another part, there will be a fracture in the body.

This chapter describes churches that were sometimes fractured by cultural and psychological influences that left believers disconnected from one another. If we stopped our review of first-century Christianity at this point, it might be discouraging. But, it is important to remember that during this period of time, the church expanded out of Judea, through Asia Minor, on into Greece, and even into Rome. God was still working despite human weaknesses. He was empowering believers to heal the fractures in the churches, and that empowerment is available to churches today.

III

PRESCRIPTIONS FOR UNITY IN THE NEW TESTAMENT CHURCH

WHEN THE FRACTURES DESCRIBED in the previous chapter occurred in churches, God had prescriptions available to heal the church and to continue the spreading of the gospel. Those prescriptions are still valid for churches today. Regardless of the reasons why fractures occur in a local congregation, we can find at least three general prescriptions in Scripture to restore unity in the church. This is not an exhaustive list of God's prescriptions for healing the church, but these three items form a solid beginning point for building unity in the Body of Christ.

1. Understand the Importance of Harmonious Relationships among Members of the Body of Christ

From Genesis to Revelation, God has revealed the importance of right relationships among His people. What's more, God has taught us that a right relationship with Him is the foundation for building strong relationships with other people. Positive relationships among members of the Body of Christ are crucial to the health of the church. Paul addressed that principle with the church at Ephesus in **Ephesians 2:13–16 [NIV]**.

> **Remember that at one time you (Gentiles) were separate from Christ, excluded from citizenship in Israel and foreigners to the covenants of the promise, without hope and without God in the world. But now in Christ Jesus you who once were far away have been brought near through the blood of Christ. For He, Himself, is our peace who has made the two one and has destroyed the barrier, the dividing wall of hostility by abolishing in His flesh the law with its commandments and regulations. His purpose was to create in Himself one new man out of the two, thus making peace, and in this one body to reconcile both of them to God through the cross, by which He put to death their hostility.**

Paul was very open when he addressed the fractures happening in churches due to cultural differences. He reminded the Ephesians that the "wall of hostility" that had existed between Jews and Gentiles had been broken down by Christ. Christ was able to accomplish something the Jewish law was incapable of doing. The redemptive love of Christ is stronger than any legal document or peace treaty. Let's look at two situations to illustrate that point.

- Two individuals quarrel over an issue, and one sues the other. After the judge or jury hears the evidence, a legal ruling is handed down. This legal finding with its accompanying documentation may resolve the legal issue, but it doesn't always end the feelings of hostility in the people involved—even if both parties agree to abide by the ruling.

- Two nations go to war over a territorial dispute. When one nation surrenders and warfare ceases, the hostile attitudes that people in these nations have toward one another probably doesn't cease—at least not for a while.

Hostility is rarely eradicated by legal or political documents. There must be a change of heart in the individuals or groups involved in order for hostility to subside. Peace for all people was achieved by Christ on the cross. Paul pointed out that Jews and Gentiles could both be a part of the Body of Christ, and they were no longer divided by the conditions of Jewish law. If something as ingrained in the lives of the Jewish people as the Mosaic law could be set aside to alleviate interpersonal differences, then other cultural differences can also be set aside for the sake of unity.

Paul brought these principles about overcoming hostility through Christ's love to a more personal level when he wrote his letter to Philemon, a strong leader in the church at Colossae. One of Philemon's slaves (Onesimus) had run away and met Paul, who was imprisoned in Rome. After Paul had led Onesimus to the Lord, he wrote to Philemon. Philemon had a legal claim to this lifelong slave that included the right to punish him severely, but Paul letter was a heart-to-heart appeal for Philemon to accept Onesimus back as a brother in Christ. The hostility between slave and owner had a basis in law, but was resolved in love as Paul noted in **Philemon 1:8–9a [NIV]**:

> **Therefore, although in Christ I could be bold and order you to do what you ought to do, yet I appeal to you on the basis of love**

A right relationship with God is possible only by loving Christ and accepting Him as Savior and Lord (**John 14:6**). When people truly love Christ, they will love others for whom He died, and they will be able to work together as the fully functioning Body of Christ. Paul taught the importance of this principle in **I Corinthians 1:10 [NIV]**:

> *I appeal to you, brothers, in the name of our Lord Jesus Christ, that all of you agree with one another so that there may be no divisions among you and that you may be perfectly united in mind and thought.*

There is a possibility that some people might misunderstand Paul's concept of "united in mind and thought." God does not ask Christians to be identical to each other. Unity can and should exist in the midst of diverse people. This interaction of diversity and unity can be seen in the various instruments in an orchestra. In my undergraduate studies at a liberal arts college, I was required to take a course in the Fine Arts curriculum, and I chose Music Appreciation. One aspect of the course required the students to listen to recordings of instruments being played and to identify them. There were some radically different sounds represented on those recordings. Although the instruments in an orchestra make different sounds, they can produce great musical harmony when they are put together properly. I believe that illustrates Paul's concept of "same mind and thought." Diverse believers can work together in harmony when they think and act in accordance with God's Word.

Paul also taught the Corinthian believers an important lesson about the things they shared in their relationships with each other. Harmonious relationships among believers involve more than interacting socially. The Holy Spirit facilitates unity among believers that is centered on spiritual outcomes. Believers receive different spiritual gifts that enable them to minister to others and fulfill God's mission for the church.

I Corinthians 12:4–6 [NIV]

> **There are different kinds of gifts, but the same Spirit. There are different kinds of service, but the same Lord. There are different kinds of working, but the same God works in all of them in all men.**

Some of the fractures in the church at Corinth arose over disagreements about who had the best spiritual gifts, and that amounts to trying to determine who was most spiritual. As a professor at a Bible college for a number of years, I occasionally heard those kinds of assessments being made by people who wanted to secure funding and to recruit students for Christian colleges. In most cases, the standards used to judge spirituality tended to be arbitrary and subjective. While it is essential that believers have spiritual accountability, the rhetoric of "We are more spiritual than they are" does not honor Christ and it fractures His body. From the first century to the twenty-first century, those assertions hinder Christian unity. Paul taught the Corinthians (and us) how senseless those kinds of comparisons are. Paul indicated that God works in different ways with different people, but those people are still united because the same God is at work in all of them.

God's Kingdom is designed to meet a wide variety of human needs since it is intended for all nations, as Jesus declared in what is known as the *Great Commission* (**Matthew 28:19–20**). Those different needs are met through diverse gifts and services that occur when the members of the Body of Christ are connected and are working in coordination with the head of the body, Jesus Christ. It is important to understand that unity is not the same thing as uniformity. Uniformity speaks to how we are expected do things just alike.

Athletics is an area where uniformity is important. At a football game, the players on each team wear the same kind of uniform, and playing rules regulate how each player must wear the uniform properly. Uniformity in the church is prescribed by God in Scripture. In regard to those commands, believers are expected to think and act just alike. In matters not covered by biblical commands; uniformity should not be demanded in the church.

Paul emphasized that having unity with diverse people was possible when believers recognized that God is the Creator who provides the gifts that are needed to mobilize diverse people to carry out the mission of the church.

Ephesians 4:3–6 [NIV]

> **Make every effort to keep the unity of the Spirit through the bond of peace. There is one body and one Spirit—just as you were called to one hope when you were called—one Lord, one faith, one baptism, one God and Father of all, who is over all and through all and in all.**

There is One God who is working in all believers. There are diverse believers who are serving One Lord. There is One Spirit who is the source of the various gifts given to diverse people.

2. Display the Mindset of Christ in All of Our Thoughts and Actions

After Christians understand that their relationships with each other are important individually and corporately, we need to look to Christ as our model for developing God-honoring relationships. We know from Scripture that Christ is the head of the church. Going back to an earlier reference to physiology, we find that it is important for human body parts to receive and to respond to messages sent from the brain. There are serious physical problems when messages from the brain are not delivered properly to the rest of the body. On several occasions, Paul taught that each member of the Body of Christ needs to carry out the messages received from the head of the church by exhibiting the "mindset of Christ" in all their thoughts and actions. Paul focused the attention of his readers on how a person acts when he or she exhibits the mindset of Christ in **Philippians 2:1–5 [NIV]**.

> If you have any encouragement from being united with Christ, if any comfort from His love, if any common sharing with the Spirit, if any tenderness and compassion, then make my joy complete by being like-minded, having the same love, being one in spirit and of one mind. Do nothing out of selfish ambition or vain conceit. Rather, in humility value others above yourselves, not looking only to your own interests, but each of you to the interests of others. In your relationships with one another, have the same mindset as Christ Jesus.

In this passage, Paul described the kind of mindset that Christ wants the members of His body to possess. We are to be tender, compassionate, and loving toward other people. We are to work with other believers agreeably as we pursue the singular purpose of being Christlike. We are not to be self-absorbed—trying to impress other people with our attributes. Those characteristics make it more likely that we will humbly take interest in other people, and not fixate on our own interests. Those are indeed the attitudes that Christ displayed in His life and revealed in His teachings.

One of the best ways to be certain that we are exhibiting the mindset of Christ is to develop such a close relationship with Him that we "clothe" ourselves in Him. Paul taught that principle to the Galatian believers in **Galatians 3:26–28 [NIV]**.

> You are all sons of God through faith in Christ Jesus, for all of you who were baptized into Christ have clothed yourselves with Christ. There is neither Jew nor Greek, slave nor free, male nor female. For you are all one in Christ Jesus.

It is obvious that people do not lose their gender or their cultural heritage when they become Christians. When we put on Christ, we operate with His mindset, and human distinctions just do not matter like they used to. From infancy onward, humans learn new ideas by contrasting similarities and differences to what they already know. On a cultural level, we learn to interact with new people by constructing categories in which to place those people—noting how similar or different they are to us. Some categories are objective and superficial such as hair color and height. Other categories are more subjective and cut more deeply into the fabric of human relationships. Those categories (such as race, ethnicity, gender, or SES) often carry value judgments that elevate or denigrate people in those categories. Those value judgments about differences among people can create fractures in the Body of Christ. We need to remember that those categories may describe human characteristics (fairly or unfairly), but they do not define people as individuals or as groups. Paul stressed that a Christian is defined by his or her relationship with Christ, and not by human-generated categories. All Christians who are "clothed in Christ" are unified in His way of thinking and acting toward other people.

3. Develop Spiritual Maturity to Prevent or Repair Fractures in the Church

New Testament writings teach Christians how to prevent fractures from developing in the Body of Christ, and they also instruct Christians how to repair fractures when they exist. Neither prevention nor repair is an easy task. Both tasks require spiritual maturity in order to be accomplished. Spiritual maturity involves a lifelong process directed by the indwelling Holy Spirit. It doesn't happen all at once, and different people mature at different rates. But we do know that, as a Christian matures, he or she will be increasingly able to live harmoniously with others even when there is tension or stress within the Body of Christ. I believe that Christians are always in the process of maturing. We never reach *"the whole measure of the fullness of Christ"* (**Ephesians 4:13**) in this life, but we need to pursue it daily.

The Book of Jude may be small in the number of verses it contains, but it is full of wisdom for Christian living. Jude wrote a concise repair manual for fractured relationships among members of the Body of Christ in **Jude 20–23a [NLT]**.

> **But you, dear friends, must build each other up in your most holy faith, pray in the power of the Holy Spirit, and await the mercy of our Lord Jesus Christ, who will bring you eternal life. In this way, you will keep yourselves safe in God's love. And you must show mercy to those whose faith is wavering. Rescue others by snatching them from the flames of judgment.**

Jude wrote that Christians who are mature in their faith have a responsibility to build up (i.e., edify) other believers in their spiritual growth. When mature believers meet those whose faith is weak, there are several courses of action they can follow, but the goal is always to build up other people—not to tear them down or build up yourself.

One course of action is to show mercy to people who have doubts and are confused about their faith. The Greek word for *mercy* is sometimes translated as "having compassion." The word *compassion* literally means that we "feel along with" the other person. The goal here is to try to make a personal connection with that person in order to direct him or her to the right path back to God. Believers possessing spiritual maturity should not condemn others for their lack of spiritual maturity. John McArthur, Pastor of Grace Community Church in Los Angeles, has aptly written on the "Grace to You" website that, "The Church needs to be a safe place for people to search and struggle spiritually." A spiritually mature believer has likely faced spiritual struggles in varying degrees, and they have learned how to grow with God's help. Pretending that we don't struggle stifles our growth toward spiritual maturity, and it can disconnect us from people who admit their struggles. Additionally, if struggling people believe they are surrounded by people who appear to have always been mature spiritually, they will likely be intimidated and not seek help from fellow believers. Those who have experienced the grace of God in their lives to overcome doubts and difficulties need to be involved in sharing that Good News in an understanding way with those who are struggling. God continues to give grace long after a believer's spiritual rebirth, and God often uses other believers to be conduits of His grace.

Sometimes, spiritually mature Christians need to take stronger measures when someone in the church has gone astray from God's Word, and is creating fractures in the Body of Christ. Jude wrote that some situations call for rescue measures. Some translations use the word *snatch* in place of *rescue*, and either word provide an accurate description of this process. The Greek word used for *rescue* or *snatch* conveys the idea of pulling strongly or persuading powerfully. Jude wrote that this kind of action was needed to save people from the "flames of judgment." This rescue action is not done as an act of condemnation, but rather as a strong attempt to restore health to members of the Body of Christ. It is comparable to a doctor setting a broken wrist or performing surgery on a broken hip. There is pain before and after the medical intervention as the rehabilitation process progresses. Spiritual interventions done with a loving spirit may be painful, but the result has eternal benefits.

Imagine that you are a witness to a traffic accident in which a person is trapped in a car, and there is fear that it will catch fire. What is the appropriate course of action for you to take after you have called 911? It is obvious that just having compassion for the trapped person won't save them as you stand nearby. Yelling verbal instructions about how to exit a car isn't enough to save them. A rescuer will have to take forceful action to get the person out of that dangerous situation.

In the context of Jude's writing, spiritual maturity (directed by the Holy Spirit) enables people to know how to do the right thing for the right reason. In some situations, we need to help build up another person's faith to help them face impending struggles. In other situations, we need to show compassion to others as they deal with their struggles. In still other situations, we need to take overt actions to help rescue them from the penalty of their mistakes, and to help them deal with the consequences of that sin.

Spiritually mature Christians are better equipped to deal with interpersonal difficulties that create or aggravate fractures in the Body of Christ. Spiritual maturity develops out of the power and the presence of the Holy Spirit in a Christian's life. This helps a believer discern fractures in the fellowship of the church, and it enables that person to seek from God's Word courses of action to repair that problem. Paul provided Timothy with a set of guidelines to pass along to believers that he would lead in **II Timothy 2:23–26 [NLT]**.

> **Again, I say, don't get involved in foolish, ignorant arguments that only start fights. A servant of the Lord must not quarrel but must be kind to everyone, be able to teach, and be patient with difficult people. Gently instruct those who oppose the truth. Perhaps God will change those people's hearts, and they will learn the truth. Then they will come to their senses and escape from the devil's trap. For they have been held captive by him to do whatever he wants.**

Paul instructed Timothy that spiritually mature Christians must not participate in the foolish arguments that create fractures in the church. The Greek word for *foolish* in this passage carries the meaning of "dealing with trivial matters." Too often, the disagreements that fracture a local congregation are spawned over issues that are quite trivial. Spiritual maturity enables a believer to distinguish matters that have Kingdom significance from the trivial matters of cultural influences or personal opinions.

Paul also indicated that the arguments were *ignorant*. The Greek word used here conveys the idea of something that is senseless, or something espoused by people without adequate learning. Remember that Paul was making a statement about the argument and not about the people involved when he used the word *foolish*. In today's social media mania, interactive input is in high demand. Additionally, sports and political talk radio programs offer arenas for people to pool opinions that are often put forth without knowing important facts (thus, meeting the definition of *ignorant*). Some people bring that type of attitude with them to church.

Paul instructed Timothy not to get involved in these kinds of arguments that would detract from his gospel ministry. And Timothy was instructed to teach others to follow his example. The mission of the church is not advanced by arguments over matters of opinion that are not addressed in God's Word. Imposing personal opinions on other believers creates disconnect among the members of the church.

In this passage, Paul did more than instruct Timothy about what Christians should not do. He outlined several important things that mature Christians can do to build unity among believers. Paul reminded Timothy that he was a servant of the Lord, and that should set the tone for his behavior and for what he would teach other believers.

Paul began by teaching that Christians should be kind to everyone. The Greek word used for *kind* conveyed the idea of "being approachable." In the context of an admonition against quarreling, Paul is advocating an attitude of openness instead of a defensive entrenchment with people who want to argue about spiritual things. That attitude involves an openness to listen, but not necessarily a mandate to accept another person's points of view without consulting Scripture.

Paul introduced a great antidote to arguing and quarreling when he told Timothy that mature believers should be able to teach others. Skillful teaching of the gospel requires both adequate knowledge and a loving attitude. Sharing the gospel with others and avoiding the trivial and foolish side trips can occur both in formal and informal settings. This sound teaching can occur in a group setting or in a one-to-one conversation. This kind of teaching is able to equip people with God's knowledge so they don't have to resort to foolish and ignorant argumentation.

Paul presented Timothy a difficult task for himself and for those he would lead. Paul said that it was important to be patient with difficult people. In the midst of arguments and quarrels, difficult people seem to flourish. The first order of business for the spiritually mature person is to be certain that you are not the difficult person in your situation. It is also important not to label others as being difficult just because they don't see things from your point of view. The importance of avoiding labels is enhanced in cross-cultural settings, because those labels may indicate the existence of bias. Difficult people tend to not want to listen to reason, and they seem anchored to their opinions. For them, being right in the argument becomes more important than the well-being of the Body of Christ. Being patient with people is often more difficult than being patient with situations, because we usually get pushback from people. When we encounter a difficult situation, there is always a possibility that we can find a way to control that situation and reduce the difficulty. With difficult people, we cannot control their responses, but we still need to interact with them. That requires patience, which is a fruit of the Spirit (**Galatians 5:22**).

Finally, Paul instructed Timothy to gently instruct opponents of the truth. There are three significant issues involved in that phrase: what to do (*instruct*), to whom to do it (*opponents of the truth*), and how to do it (*gently*). The Greek word used for *instruct* is different from the word used previously for *teach*. This instruction process is similar to the process used to train and discipline a child. The spiritually mature person is given a role to instruct and guide the less mature person. Paul referred to those who needed to be instructed as "opponents of God's truth." These were the difficult people who persisted in arguing against sound teaching. Paul indicated that the process of instruction was to be carried out *gently*. This Greek word is also translated as *meek* in other New Testament passages. This word conveys the idea of power that is under control. According to William Barclay (*New Testament Words*), this was the word that Greeks used to describe Roman warhorses. Those large, powerful horses were able to be controlled with one hand by a soldier in combat. Paul indicated that the end result of this gentle instruction was to lead the opponents to come to their senses about the spiritual matter they were arguing, and to escape from Satan's control over their thoughts and actions.

When spiritually mature Christians encounter fractures in the church, they have an obligation to find remedies that will result in unity and that are consistent with Christ's plan for the church as revealed in Scripture. Spiritually mature Christians try to live each day exhibiting the mindset of Christ in all they think and do. With this kind of mindset, they recognize the importance of being connected to other believers to carry out the mission of the church. Human weaknesses will always inflict fractures on the church, but the power of the Holy Spirit who is working in the lives of mature believers enables the church to move forward under all kinds of adverse circumstances.

IV

THE CONTEMPORARY CHURCH AND CULTURE

IT IS APPROPRIATE TO revisit an assumption stated at the beginning of this book. One of the greatest challenges facing local congregations today involves securing and maintaining unity in the "white-water rapids" of rapid cultural change. If that assumption is accurate, then we could assume the likelihood that some degree of disunity (or fractures) exists in the contemporary church. We have seen that the Body of Christ in the first century suffered fractures, and New Testament writers (inspired by the Holy Spirit) proclaimed God's prescriptions to secure and maintain unity among those believers. In the second chapter, six kinds of fractures within the Body of Christ during the first century were addressed. The sources of disunity were caused by:

- Ungodly thinking
- Cross-cultural issues
- Doctrinal differences
- Socioeconomic issues
- Differing personal preferences

- Self-righteous attitudes

So, it seems appropriate to ask whether these issues faced by the first-century church exist in the Body of Christ in the twenty-first century.

Many of the contemporary fractures may look different from the New Testament situations, because the cultural influences of today are packaged in decidedly different ways than the cultural influences seen in the first century. Imagine that you buy four boxes of your favorite cookies. When you get them home you wrap one box in Christmas wrapping paper, one box in birthday wrapping paper, one box in generic wrapping paper, and the last box in a gift bag. When you set the packages on your table, they all look different. When those packages are unwrapped, however, the contents are the same. When Christians want to apply situations described in Scripture to situations in contemporary life, the root issues will be similar, but the cultural "wrappings" will be different.

I cannot think of a single organization with which I am associated that has not made diversity an articulated goal for its membership and/or leadership. Within each of those groups, however, there is no full agreement on what constitutes diversity, or how it can be achieved. Let's revisit a point that was made in the first chapter. It is more beneficial to consider pluralism rather than diversity as a goal for believers. Pluralism involves more than diversity, because pluralism involves functioning relationships among diverse people even in the face of cultural differences. The mere presence of diverse people in a group does not guarantee that those people will want to or be able to work together. Pluralistic relationships will only thrive when there is honest dialogue (both talking and listening) that leads to a real understanding of each other's cultural background and experiences. The pluralistic perspective does not require diverse people to relinquish their previous cultural backgrounds and experiences completely. In a pluralistic paradigm, there is likelihood that different points of view will remain when diverse people interact with each other, but group goals become more important than individual backgrounds. Using Paul's analogy of the Body of Christ (found in **I Corinthians 12**), toes will remain toes and knees will remain knees, and they will work together to keep the body functioning. It seems silly to suggest that toes might demand that all other parts of the body function just like they do, but that very demand occurs in local congregations when one person or group wants all others to like what they like and do what they do. Those demands usually come out of a particular cultural influence to maintain a tradition or to implement an innovation. When that type of attitude prevails, cultural disconnect will occur.

It is important for us to try to understand some of those contemporary cultural influences that affect local congregations in order to determine where disconnects might occur. If we can anticipate where possible fractures might occur in the body of Christ, we can take proactive steps to maintain the kind of unity God wants in the church. If we understand where fractures are occurring, we can do repair work with God's guidance and His resources.

When we accept the Bible as God's authoritative revelation, then we should believe that God's Word is truth in every culture and in every generation. The Holy Spirit directed Bible writers to communicate intentional messages for the initial readers in the first century. Those messages were true and were delivered in ways that made sense to the readers at that time. The packaging of those messages, however, may or may not have the same significance for other people at other times and places even though the message itself remains relevant.

The communication process includes a sender of a message and a receiver of a message among other components. The key to sound communication involves maximizing the certainty that the message that is received is the message that was sent. Good communicators know how to package (or encode) the message so it is able to be received (decoded) properly. The cultural backgrounds of the people involved in the communication process play a large role in both encoding and decoding the message. That is one of the reasons why cross-cultural communication can be challenging. At this point, I am focusing on situations in which the speaker and the listener are communicating in the same language. Obviously, the situation is more complicated when two or more languages are being spoken.

Imagine that two people want to have a friendly game of catch with a baseball. Their purpose is to keep the ball moving back and forth for as long as possible. For that to happen, several principles must be followed:

- The thrower must keep his or her eyes on the target (the receiver).
- The throw must be within the reach of the receiver—not too high and not too low.
- The throw should not be too difficult for the receiver to grasp—not too hard and not with deceptive motions.
- The receiver needs to keep his or her eyes on the ball.
- The receiver needs to reach out for the ball.

These principles are relevant to the process of good communication, either spoken or written. The message to be communicated is represented by the ball. In communication situations, there is often one or more throwers and one or more receivers. The message(s) shouldn't be sent so it goes over the receiver's head or so low that it insults the intelligence of the receiver. The message should not be sent so harshly that it hurts the receiver or so deceptively that it confuses the receiver. Receiving communication properly essentially involves being receptive to the message, listening to it and trying to internalize it into your thinking.

In cross-cultural communication, even though those people involved may desire to keep the game of "verbal catch" going, cultural differences make it difficult. Sending a message effectively requires a certain amount of awareness of what the receiver is able to receive based on his or her cultural experiences. The sender should try to encode (or package) the message in ways he or she believes can be received properly. Receivers must be able to decode (or unwrap) the message, and that requires some awareness of the sender's cultural frame of reference. When senders and receivers really don't understand each other's cultural frame of reference, communication is difficult. Nonthreatening questions to determine the cultural frame of reference of another person can facilitate bridging such cultural differences. Learning to package God's revelation properly within the pluralistic Body of Christ is essential for the church to carry out its mission today.

The process of packaging messages is an intentional process. It can be tricky, and it can lead to challenges. Let's look at an illustration to see a challenge with communication packaging. Have you ever watched a young child open Christmas presents? I remember the surprise and excitement our young children displayed as they ripped off the wrapping paper and got to the gifts they wanted. It wasn't too long after that, however, that they became more interested in playing with the boxes that contained the presents than with the presents themselves. That situation can arise in communication also. Sometimes, people pay more attention to the packaging than to the key idea that needs to be communicated. Learning to differentiate the core gospel message from the cultural wrappings in Scripture is a very important task in the contemporary church.

In His word, God's reveals Himself, He reveals who we are, and He describes how we behave (obediently and disobediently). God also reveals in Scripture how we can get back to being what He created us to be after we have disobeyed Him. In order to communicate those crucial ideas effectively, Bible writers (inspired by the Holy Spirit) had to find ways to package God's revelations in ways the readers understood. Therefore, as we apply situations in the New Testament church to the contemporary church, we need to determine if the biblical passages are prescriptive or descriptive in nature. *Prescriptive passages* contain God's truth that is valid everywhere at all times. It is God prescribing what people need to know and do. *Descriptive passages* contain descriptions of what people did in a certain place at a certain time. Those passages may even contain descriptions about human behavior that are obviously not what God prescribes. God is very candid about what humans are capable of doing—even people who have a relationship with Him. As we study a biblical passage, we need to discern whether that passage tells us what happened, or what should happen. And we need to know that difference in order to understand and apply that Scripture properly to our lives.

Descriptive passages are prevalent in the Old Testament. For example, polygamy was not God's prescribed model for the family, yet the Bible shows us that many men had multiple wives and concubines. Obviously, the sins of great leaders like David and Solomon are not prescriptions for how God's people ought to live. Embedded in biblical descriptions of how people lived and acted are prescriptive principles about God's will that need to be understood. We need to discover God's prescriptive message for that situation rather than try to emulate the specified behaviors that are described. The New Testament also contains both prescriptive and descriptive passages. Let's look at several New Testament passages about the church, and try to determine if they are examples of descriptive or prescriptive passages.

Descriptive or Prescriptive Passages?

- **Acts 2:44–45 [NIV]**

THE CONTEMPORARY CHURCH AND CULTURE | 55

> **All the believers were together and had everything in common. Selling their possessions and goods, they gave to anyone as he had need.**

(**DESCRIPTIVE**) This passage of Scripture describes a commendable display of love and generosity at a critical time for the Early Church, but there is no scriptural mandate that all believers are to participate in communal living.

- I Corinthians 11:4–5 [NIV]

> **Every man who prays or prophesies with his head covered dishonors his head. And every woman who prays or prophesies with her head uncovered dishonors her head—it is just as though her head were shaved.**

(**DESCRIPTIVE**) Paul was writing to people who lived in a culture that held these views about head coverings. As we see news accounts of women in the Middle East today, we see that veils and head covering are prevalent in many areas. In fact, head coverings for women are still encouraged in some churches in America today. This was, and still is, a cultural issue and not a biblical mandate.

- Romans 16:3–5a [NIV]

> **Greet Priscilla and Aquila, my fellow workers in Christ Jesus. They risked their lives for me. Not only I, but all the churches of the Gentiles are grateful to them. Greet also the church that meets in their house.**

(**DESCRIPTIVE**) This is one of several passages indicating that the Early Church met in homes. Most public places of worship at that time were either Jewish synagogues or pagan temples. Therefore, contemporary Christians are not disobeying God by meeting in buildings designated as worship centers rather than in private homes.

- **Hebrews 10:24–25 [NIV]**

  And let us consider how we may spur one another on toward love and good deeds. Let us not give up meeting together as some are in the habit of doing, but let us encourage one another—and all the more as you see the Day approaching.

  (**PRESCRIPTIVE**) The idea of Christians meeting together regularly is valid in all cultures in every generation. Notice, however, that the methods used to motivate and encourage others are not specified, and there are no specifics given about what believers are to do when they meet together. This prescriptive message can be packaged in a variety of ways without violating God's intent.

- **Galatians 6:1–2 [NIV]**

  Brothers, if someone is caught in a sin, you who are spiritual should restore him gently. But watch yourself, or you also may be tempted. Carry each other's burdens, and in this way you will fulfill the law of Christ.

  (**PRESCRIPTIVE**) Paul communicated God's prescription for followers of Jesus to try to reconcile with disconnected brothers and sisters. This process is valid in the church everywhere and at all times, even when the causes of the disconnected fellowship vary.

The purpose for this exercise into understanding communication theory is to set some parameters for determining how to apply New Testament issues about the church to contemporary church issues. Essentially, we need to hold on to all the prescriptions, and we need to evaluate which descriptive passages are culturally relevant and God-honoring for us to follow. Human wisdom is not always reliable to discern the difference between prescriptive and descriptive passages, because our cultural experiences can influence our judgment about those passages. Therefore, prayer and reliance on the leading of the Holy Spirit to guide our study and our practices are imperative for the Body of Christ to be effective today.

From the Day of Pentecost onward, there has always been some tension between culture and the church. People who are alienated from God by sin tend to gravitate to cultural perspectives and values that differ from God's plans for the church. That tension exists because God's plans involve placing local congregations in the midst of human life, and that is where culture operates. Culture is created and maintained by groups of people in order to preserve their ways of living. Culture enables one group to distinguish itself from other groups, and is seen in the group's beliefs, values, and symbols used for communication. Culture determines what the group considers to be appropriate behavior in various situations. As you might imagine, the placement of God's creation (the church) in the midst of human creations (such as culture) presents several challenges, and gives rise to several questions to ponder.

What is the proper balance of influence between the church and culture?

Scripture indicates that God intended for the church to influence the lives of all people—bringing them to Christ. But how much should we allow culture to influence the church and the way the church operates? That is not an easy question to answer. Some cultural influences do not conflict with biblical mandates, but other influences do. Rather than just accept cultural influences as signs of the times, those influences must be evaluated in the light of God's Word. Cultural influences (either benign or malignant in regard to the health of the church) affect both the messages and the methods of the local congregation. Every believer brings cultural influences into the activities of the church. Hopefully, every believer takes church influence into his or her culture also.

How does being "in the world but not of the world" fit into this issue?

Jesus prayed that His disciples (and all believers coming after them) would be kept safe as they lived in cultures that were antagonistic to them. Note the part of that prayer that is found in **John 17:14–17 [NIV]**.

> **I have given them Your word. And the world hates them for they are not of the world any more than I am of the world. My prayer is not that You take them out of the world, but that You protect them from the evil one. They are not of the world even as I am not of the world. Sanctify them by the truth; Your word is truth.**

Since Jesus did not advocate "taking them out of the world," it must mean that believers are to be "left in the world." Christians are expected to be God's colony living in mankind's world, and that can result in cultural tensions.

The exodus of the Israelites is an apt comparison to the functioning of the church in every generation. That may be a surprising assertion for some readers. Because of Christ, Christians have been ransomed from the slavery of sin, which is a greater miracle than liberating the Israelites from Egyptian slavery. Our lives here on earth amount to time spent "wandering in the wilderness" of an imperfect world (even though our living conditions are much better than the Israelites' conditions). Because of God's redemptive plan through Christ, believers will eventually dwell in God's Promised Land for eternity. While we are wandering in the cultures of this world, God has given the church responsibilities to carry out for the benefit of His Kingdom, and He offers resources to benefit and bless His wandering people.

How does being the "salt of the earth" and "light of the world" work in today's world?
Jesus taught that God's influence is expected to penetrate the influences of culture, and God's influence is exerted by the Body of Christ as Christians obey His word. Sometimes, Christians focus on meeting the needs of people as if the world was a one-size-fits-all entity. Each individual that we seek to influence is wrapped in their cultural backgrounds and experiences. Perhaps, we don't reach people and meet their needs more effectively because we haven't found a way to penetrate their cultural wrappings. That was the focal point of Jesus' teaching in **Matthew 5:13–16 [NIV]**.

> You are the salt of the earth. But if the salt loses its saltiness, how can it be made salty again? It is no longer good for anything, except to be thrown out and trampled by men. You are the light of the world. A city on a hill cannot be hidden. Neither do people light a lamp and put it under a bowl. Instead, they put it on its stand, and it gives light to everyone in

the house. In the same way, let your light shine before men, that they may see your good deeds and praise your Father in heaven.

Salt and light do their jobs when they penetrate their surroundings, and Christians are expected to penetrate their cultures with God's Word displayed in their lives. Let's just focus on the idea of being the "light of the world" for a moment. Followers of Jesus are examples of reflected light. We are like the moon rather than the sun. What is the source of the light we are instructed to embody? David gave an insight into that question in **Psalm 119:105 [NIV]**.

Your word is a lamp to guide my feet and a light for my path.

Light draws attention to things, so God's Word provides light for our lives, and that draws people's attention to Him. The Body of Christ in the twenty-first century is in the lighting business. That is the message the apostle John wrote in **I John 1:5–7 [NIV]**.

This is the message we have heard from Him and declare to you: God is light, in Him there is no darkness at all. If we claim we have fellowship with Him yet walk in darkness, we lie and do not live by the truth. But if we walk in the light, as He is in the light, we have fellowship with one another, and the blood of Jesus, His Son, purified us from all sin.

Light enhances vision. As my eyesight deteriorates, I find that I need more light in order to read things clearly. Scripture indicates that the world is a dark place and people need God's light in order to discern things properly. People living in the world often have difficulty seeing solutions to their problems, because they are operating in the dark. The church should be helping people see real-life solutions to their problems in spite of being surrounded by cultural influences that tend to keep people living in the darkness. When the Body of Christ is disconnected, darkness enters the fellowship and obscures our spiritual vision. It also reduces the amount of God's light that we can reflect to that dark world in that situation.

American culture depends heavily on lighted signage. Even many church signs are now equipped with LED lighting that projects messages that catch people's attention. Artificial lights are able to penetrate darkness as long as the energy source that powers the lighting is available. God has a never-ending source of energy to produce physical and spiritual light. Compare the direct light of the sun (God's creation) with lights in our cities (man's creation). We would have difficulty living without artificial lighting, so we really can't get rid of it, even though some people complain about light pollution. Unless a person is standing in a sparsely populated part of the world, artificial lighting tends to obscure seeing stars (another of God's creations). Cultural lighting in the world that captivates our attention may keep us from seeing important spiritual things that God wants us to see. It is regrettable that the artificial lights of our culture capture people's attention, and can offset the light that the contemporary church is expected to radiate from God.

People learn how to live in this world by learning their culture, and that includes its linguistic expressions and its value systems. Because of innovations in transportation and communication, America is influenced by multiple cultures. The rallying cry of "return to traditional values" expresses concern from people who are confronted with new and different cultural influences that they don't understand. Life was easier to understand when we lived in neighborhoods where people looked like us, believed like us, and acted like us, for the most part. Those living conditions were possible before transportation and communication advances brought tremendous changes to our patterns of interaction. America's population is made up of people, from a variety of racial and ethnic backgrounds, who live and interact with one another. Our comfort foods have become noticeably multicultural as we drive by restaurants that advertise pizza, Tex-Mex, Chinese, Thai, and many other food choices. We live with different languages being spoken around us, and we remember the days when language differences referred to accents and dialects from another part of this country.

Based on their cultural backgrounds and experiences, people form distinctive points of view about life and about their roles in that way of living. But that is not just a twenty-first century development. The apostle Paul experienced that personally, and he shared with the believers in Corinth how his perspectives had changed as we read in **II Corinthians 5:16–17 [NIV]**.

> **So, from now on we regard no one from a worldly point of view. Though we once regarded Christ in this way, we do so no longer. Therefore, if anyone is in Christ, he is a new creation; the old has gone, the new has come.**

What are some "worldly points of view" that are used to "regard" people today?

Many of our initial reactions to other people are based on our perceptions of beauty, body type, skin color, and signs of wealth—just to name a few categories. Those initial perceptions are usually culturally based and often the basis for how we choose to interact (or not interact) with certain people. Our personal preferences about people and things are often based on human points of view only, and that can promote cross-cultural biases in local congregations.

Paul admitted that his initial attitudes about Jesus were based strictly on human value judgments. I don't believe that Paul was the only person who has done that very thing. It is important for believers in America to ponder how Christ (and the church) is regarded in our world today, and how Christians regard other people. The answers to these kind of questions can impact how effective the church will be in this world.

- Will believers be disconnected or unified?
- Do we limit our evangelism to certain people because of our human points of view?
- Are we cautious about proclaiming our new life in Christ because other people regard Christ and His followers from a human point of view and they might be offended?

It is possible to develop a sense of inferiority about being a follower of Christ in a world that expresses disdain for all things Christian. One response to this feeling is to refrain from doing or saying things that draw attention to our Christian faith. With God's help, we can change our viewpoints like Paul did, and regain healthy feelings about our commitment to Christ. Once we get our perspective on living in line with God's value system, the value judgments of the world lose their impact on us.

It is also possible to develop a sense of superiority about being a follower of Christ in a world that expresses disdain for all things Christian. Such a feeling of superiority often originates in the belief that the church life we experienced in the formative years of our spiritual development must be THE proper church life now. These believers might dig their heels in and demand that anyone who wants to be a part of their fellowship must adhere to the ways of conducting church that is a part of their experience bank. Since most people attending any given church have had different experiences in their spiritual development, some degree of disconnection is likely to occur when this attitude prevails.

Living in a world with multiple cultural influences may seem like a roller coaster ride—thrilling, scary, full of ups and downs. But imagine trying to master a Hula-Hoop while riding that roller coaster. That is comparable to what happens when we add the increased speed of cultural change to our discussion of cultural influences. By the way, if your cultural experiences don't include knowledge of the Hula-Hoop, you could google it to get my point.

V

UNDERSTANDING CULTURAL CHANGE IN THE CONTEMPORARY CHURCH

LET'S BEGIN THIS CHAPTER on cultural change with an illustration. A factory has been very successful making a particular product for over thirty years. A review of the company's finances and its inventory reveals that business is stagnant and beginning to decline. The leadership team meets to discuss finding new ways to impact their manufacturing marketplace, and there are rather strong discussions about making changes. Some leaders are proud of their past, and the legacies of those who preceded them in the business. Other leaders believe that the very life of the business is dependent on making changes. After a time, the owners agree that changes in their business plan are needed, and they begin an even more difficult process as they try to figure out how to expand their business in new directions. After more discussions and research provided by outside consultants, the owners decide on the new products they will be manufacturing, and new ways to improve what they have been manufacturing. A marketing survey indicates that these production changes will be attractive to an increased market of buyers. This pushes these business people into a really difficult decision-making process of determining what machinery must be added to make the changes, and what machines must be modified or discarded because they are no longer useful.

The activities in this illustration are seen in many local congregations as their leaders take a look at the work of their congregation in a culturally disconnected environment. The mission for the Body of Christ as revealed in Scripture is the "business plan" for a local congregation. It is a stewardship responsibility of leaders in each congregation to regularly review how well that business plan is working. Please understand that such a review goes well beyond attendance figures and how well the budget is being met. A "Great Commission Assessment" is necessary to determine how effectively the congregation is making disciples (both evangelism and discipleship) in a world of diverse cultural influences. That assessment also involves determining whether fractures due to cultural disconnect are happening in the Body of Christ that assembles there.

A study of Scripture reveals that God's Kingdom is eternally victorious, but we also know that the church faces challenges in this world. The Body of Christ is called to impact cultures *positively* (according to God's standards) even while it is being impacted by cultural influences negatively. It is important to understand whose impact is greater, and why that is so. The church is under attack from a number of outside forces (instigated by Satan) as the American society (with its multiple cultures) continues to become less receptive to Christian thoughts and expressions. But there are also conflicts within the structures of our local congregations that are also instigated by Satan, and those conflicts may be more challenging than the outside forces. Sometimes, the internal conflicts are disguised for a while because the people use similar religious words and participate in similar church practices despite actually being culturally divided from one another.

For example, several members of a congregation talk among themselves about the preacher dressing too casually on Sunday morning to suit their preferences. They continue attending services and they continue stating their concerns to an increasing number of fellow members. At some point, they find that some other church members say they like the way the preacher dresses. In this situation, individual believers or groups of believers struggle with one another holding the belief that they, alone, are spiritually correct. As these internal differences become more overt, factions develop and the Body of Christ becomes fractured

Believers who should be connected spiritually as members of the Body of Christ find themselves separated from one another because of their cultural differences. The existence of different cultural influences in a congregation does not automatically produce fractures in the body of believers. But, when Christians allow cultural differences to become more important than the unity that Jesus wants in His church, there is a likelihood of a fracture. In these cultural struggles within the church, Christians may be forced to decide whether they love cultural things more than they love Jesus. That is a deceptive choice point. Most of us don't come to an intellectual intersection where we consciously choose to turn down Culture Avenue instead of staying on Jesus Way. Cultural enticements are often seductive and they appear to offer what we need and want spiritually. Sometimes, our powers of rationalization convince us that leaving Jesus Way to go down Culture Avenue really won't be a problem for us spiritually in the long run.

What might cause people in a local congregation to experience cultural disconnect? Perhaps they have resided in different nations, or in different geographical areas of this country, or there may be rural–urban–suburban differences. Maybe they have different family backgrounds, and that often accounts for different religious experiences in the past. A growing source of cultural disconnect in the contemporary church arises among people who grew up in different cultural eras, and possess different attitudes about changes in cultural practices and values.

Cultural disconnect can have a profound effect on religious beliefs, moral values, and cultural expressions. In regard to our beliefs, cultural influences can impact how we interpret Scripture. The question asked of Jesus—"Who is my neighbor?"—has great significance for the contemporary church. I believe that question forces twenty-first century Christians to confront some difficult choices about the church because of cultural disconnect. Jesus' story of the Good Samaritan highlighted cultural disconnect between Jews and Samaritans, and taught that any person in need is worthy to be considered a neighbor. In our local congregations, there are cultural influences that separate people and make it difficult for Christians to live with Christ's expanded definition of a neighbor. The concept of neighbor may not be meaningful to people from certain areas in America where the concept of neighborhood seems to be lost. People from other areas of the country, where the concept of neighborhood is alive and well, are comfortable because those neighborhoods are composed mostly of people who are culturally similar to them. When those geographic neighborhoods experience demographic changes, the concept of "neighbor" may change. Our teaching and preaching need to give attention to identifying and emphasizing the importance of connections that can enable us to live in a culturally diverse world as the neighbors Jesus had in mind.

Cultural disconnect is evident in the differences that people in America have over moral values. This disconnect can lead to fractures in a local congregation when some people's moral values have been influenced by our relativistic culture while others adhere to God's absolutes as found in the Bible. A *relativistic culture* is defined as one in which moral decision-making is based on each culture determining what is right and wrong. Cultural relativism was not created in America, but we have advanced the concept considerably. The Bible tells us in **Judges 17:6 [NLT]** that the people of Israel experienced this.

In those days Israel had no king; all the people did whatever seemed right in their own eyes.

In 1966, Joseph Fletcher introduced the concept of situational ethics. Fletcher's premise was that moral decision-making would vary from situation to situation. A major thrust of his argument was that if a person's goal is justified, then any method to reach that goal is morally acceptable. This line of thinking eradicated reliance on most all absolute standards when making moral judgments. Situational ethics was one of the roots from which today's relativistic viewpoint has grown. When that thinking infiltrates the Body of Christ, factions can develop between absolutists and relativists. Actually, there are usually more than two factions since there are many degrees of relativism. There are people who want to hold on to some traditional moral values, but are willing to forego others because of cultural change. The ratio of traditional values to situational values held by individuals in a congregation may vary considerably. That mixture of traditional and situational values in a church often leads people to try to explain away biblical prescriptions that don't mesh with their cultural experiences. Let's take this discussion of traditional values a little further. Christians need to be certain the traditional values they champion are actually biblical values. Most adults today have lived through the evolution of relativism over the past fifty years. It is possible that some of our traditional values may have been influenced by our cultural experiences and we are not aware of that. Followers of Christ need to constantly cross-reference our beliefs with biblical support.

Without adherence to moral absolutes that originate with God, our culture has become very unstable. Other belief systems have developed that urge people to separate facts (i.e., science) and faith (i.e., religion), and science is seen as the answer to life's problems by many people. Under the flag of diversity (which is not a bad thing in and of itself) came the idea that each person could have his or her own ideas on morality, because each person could have his or her own supreme being. Some people see themselves as the "supreme being" in their lives, while others place materialism in that position. Therefore, developing a systematic set of absolute moral values has been deemed inappropriate by these people.

I have been emphasizing the importance of developing unity with people who are disconnected due to different experiences and different beliefs. There has been a stress that pluralism is more than diversity, because pluralism involves healthy relationships among diverse people even in the face of cultural tension. The mere presence of diverse people does not guarantee that those groups will want to or be able to work together in unity. Now, we have arrived at topics that will require some people to adjust their preferences and beliefs to bring them into obedience to God's Word. The Body of Christ must answer to its head, Jesus Christ. That is how all the body parts stay together and function properly.

Christians must be vigilant when discerning whether cultural relativism has influenced the message and methods of a church. Several websites publish a quote attributed to C.H. Spurgeon, theologian and preacher, that defines *discernment* and gets to the heart of the subtle issues that arise when cultural relativism becomes a part of a congregation. Spurgeon said: "Discernment *is not simply a matter of telling the difference between right and wrong; rather, it is knowing the difference between the right and the almost right.*" Sometimes, the pathways of almost right are enticing because of cultural packaging, and that leads some Christians away from biblical values and creates fractures in the Body of Christ. In the next several chapters, we will look at three specific aspects of church life that are affected by cultural disconnect.

- Expectations of the church
- Methods used in the church
- Proclaiming the message of the church

VI

CULTURAL DISCONNECT IN THE EXPECTATIONS OF THE CHURCH

BELIEVERS IN THE CONTEMPORARY church can become disconnected because they have experienced different cultural expressions in worship styles, clothing styles, and language usage over their lifetimes. Those prior experiences often create expectations about what should happen at church. That last phrase may be a critical part of the disconnect discussion. When we focus on going to church rather than being the church, we are more vulnerable to challenges when cultural influences affect a local congregation. While attention will be given to different opinions about church methodology later in this book, some thought can be given to it now. Traditional views about church methods tend to include more formality in both the proper clothing worn to church and the proper way for worship services to be conducted. There is a general cultural evolution toward informality in most areas of life in America and that influences what is done in local congregations today. When people expect that only their views on formality or informality in the church should be followed, then disconnect is likely to occur. Cultural disconnect can also occur over religious language and the style of preaching and teaching. For a number of years, debates have occurred over the best or the only translation of the Bible that should be used. Now, people decide whether they will read from a print edition of the Bible, a smartphone, or a tablet. Since American culture has developed more informal ways of communication, it is not surprising that disconnect has occurred in local congregations over ways to proclaim Scripture and the genre of music to be used.

Cultural disconnect can be seen in differing views about what needs people expect a local congregation to fulfill, and how they believe the congregation should carry out its functions. Christians and non-Christians alike have a variety of expectations about what a church building should look like, and how a local congregation should function. Individuals who are not influenced by traditional religious experiences are often attracted to congregations that look and act like other institutions in contemporary culture. Many local congregations meet in storefront buildings or former theatres because those leaders believe "seekers" will be more comfortable in surroundings they visit throughout the week. People who are not influenced by traditional religious experiences are also attracted to congregations whose musical expressions are similar to the entertainment style they prefer.

In some people's minds, the concept of the Body of Christ (church as an organism) has been replaced by corporate business models prominent in our culture (church as an organization). Should the church operate as an organism or an organization? Can a local congregation have corporate structure and still function as an organism? A key question is whether those decisions about the organizational model of the local congregation are based on cultural expectations or on the most effective way for the church to grow in the twenty-first century. There is no question that state and federal legal systems in

America require churches to operate with organizational accountability. Tax laws and labor laws require local congregations to be organized, and they can be held accountable if they do not adhere to those laws. In the organizational model, emphasis is placed on organizational growth and efficiency, which sounds like a reasonable goal. However, there are some pitfalls that need attention as a local congregation pursues the organizational model. The development of a sound organizational structure does not guarantee that the needs of people in the congregation are being met. In the organizational model, people may spend more time "polishing the machinery" of the organization than using that machinery to meet the needs of the people. On the other hand, having a strong organizational structure does not preclude a local congregation from fulfilling its role as the Body of Christ in today's world. It is a matter of making the biblical mission of the church the driving force for what the congregation does.

God wants the Body of Christ to grow quantitatively (evangelism) and qualitatively (spiritual growth), and that can occur in a variety of ways. The Bible provides many examples of incredible church growth in the first century, and that growth occurred when the Holy Spirit brought people in need to meet Jesus at the cross. That basic formula for church growth is still valid today, and can occur with a variety of congregational models and in congregations of varying sizes. Whether we talk about the *church universal* (i.e., the Body of Christ) or a particular local congregation, we may be thinking about a monolithic entity. That is, we think in terms of groups of people without giving attention to the diverse individuals who make up those groups. This is not an either-or situation, because the quest for unity involves considering groups of people and individuals. When members of a local congregation are entrenched in their differing expectations about what the church should be and how it should carry out its mission, they are likely to become disconnected from one another. Sometimes, believers become judgmental about churches that operate differently from the church they attend. The Body of Christ can take many forms to carry out God's mission. Some forms receive more attention than others, but all are needed for the entire Body of Christ to function properly. It is important to have respect for the ministries carried out in megachurches, in small inner-city or rural congregations, and in congregations in between.

Cultural disconnect also occurs in local congregations in regard to changing expectations about relationships among the believers. Dr. Rachna Jain (2010) suggested that people in the twenty-first century confuse digital intimacy with true intimacy. Social media appears to give people a connection to a great number of people in rapid fashion, but the level of true intimacy may be minimal. An increasingly problematic part of digital intimacy is that many people appear to be satisfied to settle for superficial interaction in their relationships. Today's emphasis on instant messaging promotes impersonal communication. I have seen examples of people whose offices are located next to each other communicating with one another through emails and text messages rather than walking a few feet to talk face-to-face. People lament that they don't know people in their residential neighborhoods any more. Customer service in the business world seems to be a lost art with few attempts made to develop anything more than superficial interaction between buyer and seller. Technological innovations are not going away, but people must not let these tools restructure important aspects of their personal and social lives. Carrying out daily life in an impersonal culture can carry over to relationships in the church. In order to ensure unity in the Body of Christ, Christians must find ways to develop meaningful personal interaction with other believers. That will require intentional steps to offset the cultural influences of impersonal lifestyles.

This book is being written after an extended time of social distancing due to the COVID-19 pandemic. Worship services have been modified and disseminated through a variety of electronic media. The comments I have read and heard are quite diverse. Some local congregations did not follow governmental restrictions because they believed (for several reasons) that the traditional ways of worship needed to be practiced. Other individuals in those congregations chose not to attend church activities in person.

Some individuals recognized that electronic transmissions of worship services were necessary even though they would rather worship together with other believers. Individuals whose experiences included a lot of exposure to electronic and digital meetings and communication had little discontent with the changes. An interesting question in the minds of some people involves how people will react the farther we get from the time of restrictions. Will people return to face-to-face contact and to familiar ways of worship, or will they have grown accustomed to distance worshipping via electronic media?

Another area where expectations about the church can lead to cultural disconnect involves political issues. Some Christians expect their local church to be overtly involved in political issues. Religious groups have become prime fodder for political polling mills on a regular basis. That is why so many candidates for state and national offices make campaign stops at worship services. The "Religious Right" has been praised or vilified depending on who is speaking, but its presence is known. However, this one-size-fits-all label applied to the church's involvement in political issues is misleading. It should be obvious that all Christians in America do not believe the same things politically (although I have some acquaintances who doubt that anyone can be a Christian and belong to the "other" political party). The injection of divisive political issues into the life of a congregation enhances the possibility of cultural disconnect and creates fractures in the fellowship of those believers. That can distract believers from the mission of the church by putting resources to use for projects or programs not related to the biblical purposes of the church.

An important issue in this discussion is to consider whether believers are involved in political activism in order to influence the culture for Christ, or are involved as a response to retaining familiar cultural views and values? Are these believers trying to sustain the mission of God's Kingdom or sustain cultural interests? As the American society becomes more polarized and there is a general decline in social civility, a congregation must prayerfully consider both its involvement in political issues and the behavior its members exhibit while involved in political issues. A culturally influenced church may find itself backing a candidate on cultural values rather than discovering his or her views on spiritual matters. When a government's primary function is seen as the distribution of benefits to citizens, then it is tempting to back a candidate who you believe will distribute the benefits your way. When a body of believers takes a stand on a political issue, that stand needs to be based on prescriptions that God has revealed in His Word. Individual Christians have a right to their political views and their views on social values that lie outside Scripture, but those views should not be allowed to produce fractures in the Body of Christ. "Speaking the truth in love" (**Ephesians 4:15**) is a biblical prescription that covers all cultures and all situations.

In the midst of cultural disconnect, Christians from differing cultural backgrounds find that life in a local congregation can be challenging when their expectations for the church aren't met. Jonathan Merritt in *Learning to Speak God from Scratch* (2018) suggests that Christians often resort to one of three responses when their expectations for the church are challenged by cultural change. He termed the first response *"fossilization."* These responders adamantly stay where they have been traditionally. They are entrenched in traditional, sacred vocabulary and methods. This approach is easier (and more comfortable) than trying to solve the challenges that multicultural social change brings. Fossilization arises out of a belief that the culture that was experienced in the past is the only type of culture in which to conduct the work of the church today.

Merritt refers to the second response option as *"substitution."* The substitution category is often comprised of people who do not have traditional experiences in the church. These people often bring their views and values from the larger culture, and they want to substitute new approaches that resonate with them. Since their experiences often come from experiences marked by rapid cultural change, these substitution advocates lobby for immediate changes, because they are not satisfied with their current religious experiences.

When the views of substitution advocates prevail and social change influences church activities, people with traditional roots feel uncomfortable. They go through the motions of accepting change, but they still harbor some level of discontent. When people from traditional backgrounds become disillusioned with the "substitution" perspective, they often revert to the "fossilization" category—thinking those are the only options they have. These differing views about change as expressed in fossilization and substitution can lead to fractures in the Body of Christ, because there does not appear to be a middle ground.

It is important to remember that trying to deny or avoid challenges of cultural change impacting the church does not resolve those challenges. Traditional words and ideas cannot be avoided totally if a church is Bible-based. We need to remember that there is no "Gospel 2.0." The essentials of God's Word prevail over any and all cultural change.

Merritt suggests a third response option that he terms *"transformation."* People in this category forge new paths to achieve biblical goals for the church. This approach begins with the realization that language and methodology may fluctuate over time, and that doesn't necessarily destroy God's intentions for the church. Transformationalists find ways to build unity in the Body of Christ by communicating the timeless truth of the gospel in ways that connect with people from diverse cultural backgrounds.

In a much earlier time, C. S. Lewis suggested that much of the change in the church was like new growth on trees. Lewis wrote that, "New meanings do not obliterate old ones, but are instead connected to them." (*Studies in Words*, 1960)

Merritt's concept of transformation is reminiscent of Paul's words to the Romans in **Romans 12:2 [NASV]**, and those words have never been more significant as the contemporary church moves forward in a sea of social change:

> **And do not be conformed to this world, but be transformed by the renewing of your mind, that you may prove what the will of God is, that which is good and acceptable and perfect.**

Paul wanted his readers to understand that they did not have to be locked into a particular type of culture (Jewish, Greek, or Roman). God's Kingdom, as advanced by the Body of Christ, has been empowered by the Holy Spirit since Pentecost, and that transforming power can provide the energy and guidance for the Kingdom to flourish despite cultural changes. Contemporary transformers don't let the influence of the world overshadow the gospel, but they do recognize the need to package that gospel so it will be received by people of all cultural backgrounds. This is an important realization for all people in the church today, because there is not one person today (regardless of age or circumstance) whose cultural future will be the same as their lifestyle today. Expectations built only on the past will lead to disappointment in current and future church experiences because of the inevitable flow of cultural change.

In addition to multiple cultures exerting a variety of influences on the church in America, an even greater issue today involves the rapid speed at which all those cultures are changing. Change has always been inevitable in life, both physically and socially. We have biblical support for understanding that spiritual growth always involves change. The new wrinkle in today's world is *social acceleration*—i.e., the increasingly rapid rate of social change occurring in our world. The fully functioning Body of Christ today must learn to carry out its mission in the most rapidly changing time in human history.

Take a moment to reflect on how the speed of social change has affected your life.

- Can you think of things that were important parts of the culture you lived in as a child that no longer exist?
- Can you think of any important moral values that you believe have changed over your lifetime in this culture?
- Can you think of anything about life at church today that is significantly different from the past as you remember it?

People, from teens to senior adults, can testify to changes that have occurred in their lifetimes. People, whose formative years of life were times of less rapid social change, may find the rapid changes of the twenty-first century to be discomforting. Younger people, who have grown up in times of rapid social change, tend accept those changes as a normal part of life.

Social scientists have come up with names for the cultural eras in which Americans have lived. While it is inaccurate to think that all people in any one category are alike, the differences in the experiences of people in these categories are significant. While there may be some debate over the exact age spans for these categories, the following terms seem to be the most widely accepted.

"Elders" - born before 1946

"Baby Boomers" - born in 1946–1964
"Generation X" - born in 1965–1980
"Millennials" or "Gen Y" - born in 1981–1996
"Post-Millennials" or "Gen Z" - born in 1997 to the present

Each of these eras is grouped in intervals of 15 to 18 years. It would be erroneous, however, to believe that each interval has had the same rate of social change. People in the earlier cultural eras have different relationships with change than those in more recent eras. Nostalgia is more likely to occur with people who have seen the most cultural change. Most of us feel a sense of comfort looking back on what we remember from experience, rather than looking into an unknown future of ongoing change. Rapid social change creates the idea that life should be lived in an ongoing present tense. Many Millennials see little value looking for guidance from a past that doesn't seem to exist any longer, or a future that really can't be known. The future is indeed hazy. Some futurists have suggested that children in elementary school today will take jobs as adults that do not even exist at this time. Interestingly, Alvin Toffler, in *Future Shock*, predicted the same thing in 1970.

There is a difference between living in the moment and living in an ongoing present tense. There is value in being aware (and appreciative) of life as it is being lived now. Phrases like *"stop and smell the roses"* and *"enjoy the journey as well as the destination"* encourage people to stay focused on life in the present tense. Living in the moment does not exclude lessons and memories from the past or goals and strategies for the future. Living in the ongoing present tense tends to discard the past as not useful and the future as not knowable.

A cultural battleground brought on by rapid social change occurs in attitudes about history. People who have known rapid social change most of their lives may be tempted to see little value in studying history. Looking back doesn't seem to offer much practical help in dealing with the ongoing present tense. Perhaps an even more serious issue is the tendency to view past events in terms of present values instead of viewing historical events in the context in which they happened. There have been some atrocities in American and world history. Recently, some attempts have been made to rewrite those events and/or to remove any reminders of those events from books or from historical sites. The belief that past events are irrelevant to life today or the belief that past events you disagree with should be disregarded can even have an impact on the Body of Christ.

Living in an ongoing present tense creates challenges in the church. God's truth includes a very relevant past as Christians reflect on Christ's redemptive sacrifice and the establishment of the church. When Christians believe in eternal life, they acknowledge a very relevant future. Living in the present has it virtues in many ways, but ignoring the past or the future is problematic. These time warps can create fractures in the Body of Christ at a time when Baby Boomers and Millennials (and all other believers) need to work together to further God's Kingdom through the church.

As Baby Boomers were growing up, traditions were normal and those traditions were expected to continue for subsequent generations. Tradition provided a solid footing for young people to learn how to grow up in a culture that was expected to be like the culture their parents experienced. Traditions were guidelines for appropriate behavior in order to meet the expectations of their parents and other significant adults. In today's world of social acceleration, traditional things are often viewed as an anchor that prevents progress and not an anchor of stability.

There is now an expectation that real value is found only in the new and different—and the new and different changes constantly. In the ongoing present tense, there is a perception that things become obsolete just because they are from the past. As a person who has used Word as the software-of-choice for my writing projects, I have had compatibility problems when I updated my computer.

The old software didn't work right in the new configurations. The constant upgrading that goes on with cellular phones can be mind-boggling as consumers try to keep up with each new generation that hits the market.

Have you ever had a microwave oven or some other type of small appliance that doesn't work any longer? If so, you know that repairing the appliance isn't really a viable option. If you can find a person who does repair work, the cost would likely be greater than buying a new appliance. This is an example of what happens when rapid social change feeds into the business model of planned obsolescence that manufacturers and marketers have developed. This reality has created stress for older adults who either experienced the Depression of the 1930s or were raised by parents who had experienced the Depression. People in these eras were taught to save everything because it might come in handy someday. If something was broken, it needed to be repaired rather than discarded. Thus, there was always value added to the things of the past. It is difficult for these people to understand why they should pay good money for things that are not made to last. It is possible that the church can inadvertently promote planned obsolescence under the guise of needing to stay on the cutting edge of cultural relevance. This approach emphasizes operating in the ongoing present tense in regard to church methods and messages, and that will be addressed later.

This discussion becomes even more critical when the rapid changes involve our traditional values. It is disconcerting to discover that things that were once very important to us (individually and nationally) are now considered no longer valuable. Value systems (cultural or spiritual) provide meaning for a person's life. Value systems attach price tags to things, events, and people in a culture. Some of the values only have meaning in this world, but spiritual values have meaning for now and eternity. Social change alters the price tags in life more rapidly than the pricing signs in front of your local gas station. Because of the push for change and the elimination of obsolete things, people accustomed to traditional values might even wonder if that means they are no longer valuable as people. When a local congregation no longer looks and acts like the church they remember from the past, those with traditional views can feel disconnected, and fractures appear in the Body of Christ. Changes in worship styles lead some older adults to believe their desires are not considered to be as important as those of younger people—and another crack opens up in the unity of the local congregation.

Traditional living valued the experiences gained in the past. Respect was given to older adults in a variety of situations. When the past is devalued, intergenerational relationships tend to change. In a reaction to the rapidly changing world, many older adults may develop negative attitudes about younger people whose lifestyles are significantly different from theirs. At the same time, younger people (who are accustomed to living in times of rapid cultural change) grow impatient with those who seem to be resisting change. There is, however, one constant for people in all eras of cultural change. Every generation of people in America today needs to realize that the world of their adult years will be different from the world in which they grew up. That constancy of change will continue throughout all of our lifetimes, and the speed of those changes will not likely slow down.

Despite the realization that change is inevitable, some people are highly resistant to it. Resistance to change is not based on the calendar as much as it is on how much cultural change occurred in those years of life. On the other hand, if rapid change is all you have experienced, then you are not as likely to resist it. A major challenge for the church in the midst of social acceleration is to find ways to unite believers who have different attitudes about cultural change.

Unified (2018) is a book cowritten by US Senator Tim Scott and US Representative Trey Gowdy, two legislators from the state of South

Carolina. In a variety of ways, they address building national unity and spiritual unity. The authors have developed a strong friendship despite significant differences in their life experiences. They are racially diverse, they were raised in different parts of South Carolina, they had different work backgrounds before entering politics, and they belong to different political parties. These authors stress the importance of learning how to turn *contrasts* (differences that arise naturally out of life experiences) into *conciliation* (i.e., bringing people together despite their differences) instead of *conflict* (i.e., situations in which people have "dug in their heels" about their differences). The authors share strong Christian beliefs, and their concepts for national unity have strong implications for the church.

The concept of conciliation stressed by Senator Scott and Representative Gowdy is similar to the biblical concept of reconciliation. Unity occurs in the Body of Christ when Christians really understand and appreciate the ministry of reconciliation that Paul described in **II Corinthians 5:17–20 [NLT]**.

> **This means that anyone who belongs to Christ has become a new person. The old life is gone; a new life has begun! And all of this is a gift from God, who brought us back to Himself through Christ. And God has given us this task of reconciling people to Him. For God was in Christ, reconciling the world to Himself, no longer counting people's sins against them. And He gave us this wonderful message of reconciliation. So, we are Christ's ambassadors: God is making His appeal through us.**

Reconciliation is made possible because Jesus went to the cross to redeem humanity. God has wanted His people to be reconciled to Him from the moment of creation. Sin created separation in God's relationship with people, and He steadfastly pursued processes to reclaim His people. The Old Covenant, based on the Law, unified the Israelites to some degree; but laws make people do the right things because they have to or they will suffer a penalty. The New Covenant, based on Christ's redemptive work, invites people to share in God's Kingdom because they desire to do so. Newness in Christ is the direct result of the New Covenant God made with Christians. Life for new creations in God's Kingdom is based on relationships—to God, to Christ, and to other believers. It is important to remember that unity in the Body of Christ requires that we be reconciled to each other under Christ's headship, and that reconciliation is to occur despite our cultural differences or the speed at which things change in our lives.

VII

CULTURAL DISCONNECT IN THE METHODS OF THE CHURCH

THE FOCAL POINT OF any discussion on church methodology is usually the worship service. Before getting into the methods of worship, it is beneficial to address the meaning and purpose of *worship*. That remark may elicit a "duh, everybody knows that." But, do they? Scripture passages throughout the Bible reveal that worship involves humble adoration and praise for God. Worship is a mindset and a lifestyle first and foremost. That distinguishes your "service of worship" (**Romans 12:1**) from just attending worship services. However, the New Testament reveals the importance of corporate worship in the lives of first-century Christians. Regardless of whether we are worshipping individually or corporately, our primary focus is on God. Thoughts that are spoken or sung in those services should help us focus on God and on our relationship with Him. When the methodology used in the worship service replaces God as the focal point of our attention, we have moved away from biblical worship.

There is a great deal of discussion about the proper format for a worship service in the twenty-first century. Those discussions usually reveal a person's preferred format for a worship service; and, in the contemporary church, there are differing preferences. Those preferences reflect diverse personal experiences derived from a variety of cultural inputs. Choosing sides about the music program (band or no band, praise team or choir, hymns or praise songs) is an example of the cultural disconnect that can divide the Body of Christ. Believers need to seek an understanding about why certain people prefer particular formats, and then some discussion about how to unify people with differing preferences. The same process holds true for debating the style of preaching (power point with video or not, pulpit or not; number of points in the sermon) and the appropriate apparel for the one doing the preaching. It is interesting to note that the suit and tie for the pastor of the past has been replaced in many churches by a pastor wearing jeans and a shirt worn with the shirttail out. I suspect that is just a matter of an informal uniform replacing a more formal uniform due to current cultural influences or personal preferences of the pastor.

The personal history of each us is recorded in our memories, and we attach emotional value to those memories. Our memory banks include people and situations from every area of our lives—home, school, work, and even church. For those who have been Christians for a long time, there are memories about going to church that reach back perhaps to our childhood. Those memories include activities we experienced there, and they are associated with people (family members, friends, teachers, pastors, et. al). Those memories probably reflect how our spiritual lives were shaped to some extent, so those memories have some deep roots in our emotions as well as our minds. Some people have positive memories of prior church experiences, while others do not. Those positive or negative emotions about memories of church involve issues that impact people's attitudes about church today. People with positive memories are attracted to aspects of church life that are compatible with those memories, and the values they assign to those memories.

People who have not been involved in a church over a long period of time do not have an extensive bank of memories about church, so they are not invested in particular methodology. What some people value about traditional church methodology is not significant to newcomers—in fact, it may seem foreign to them. These different perspectives among church attenders reflect cultural disconnect that can hinder unity if they are not addressed. The "memory bank gap" in regard to church experiences can produce a disconnected environment and personal discomfort. It is common for people to try to protect themselves from feeling uncomfortable. That protection can be displayed in pressing for changes to be made in church format, or in being resistant to changing church procedures. Eventually, it can lead dissatisfied people to gravitate to groups of people in other congregations who have similar views on church methods. It sounds reasonable to say that people normally gravitate to a church where they feel more comfortable. Eventually, however, a group of homogeneous believers must confront the question about who they will evangelize. Will it just be people who share their preferences? That method of operation does not fit the biblical mandate for making disciples of all people. If the comfortable people take seriously the biblical mandates, they will be back in the realm of discomfort that they left previously.

It is important to understand how the past experiences of various people in a local congregation have shaped their opinions and preferences about how the church should operate. But once those differences are understood, then, the task is to find ways to work through those differences to build unity.

Most of the differences among people in a local congregation don't lie in their ultimate goals; these lie in the ways they think those goals should be reached. Differing views about church methodology can lead some people to feel disconnected from others in group interactions. Some people might feel threatened by changes that are occurring in the church programming. Other people are concerned that more changes aren't occurring in the church. Perhaps, if we took time to understand why other people had such different views, we could find a way to connect with each other. That can be accomplished when believers openly share their views with others and those views are respected. More importantly, unity is facilitated when members of the Body of Christ focus on things that they have in common instead of focusing on their differences. By helping Christians see that there is agreement on the goals for the work of the church, they might be more willing to look for transformational approaches to reach those goals. Transformation is a biblical concept for a type of change that is orchestrated by God. The Greek word often translated as *transformation* is found in four places in the New Testament, and can be transliterated into English as *metamorphosis*. That word was used twice in the gospel accounts of Jesus' transfiguration (**Matthew 17:2, Mark 9:2**). Paul used that word when he wrote about changes that occur in people as they mature spiritually (**Romans 12:2, II Corinthians 3:18**). A major task for Christians involves embracing the unity that comes from spiritual transformation even when it means prying ourselves away from the cultural bonds that can cause disconnect in fellowship.

The twenty-first century can be referred to as the digital age. Our digitalized culture has lessened the need for many items that were once considered indispensable—landline telephones, wristwatches, cash registers, and getting a human voice when calling a business, just to name a few. The emphasis in this digital world is directed toward communicating bite-sized ideas and using electronic imaging to get information very quickly. A friend in Michigan recounted a story that illustrates differences in people who have grown up in the digital age. My friend's preteen son has a morning ritual at breakfast of reading the sports section of the *Detroit Free Press* from top to bottom on the Internet. On a recent trip together, my friend and his son stopped to get gasoline and snacks. After Mark paid for his purchases, he noticed his son staring intently at a rack near the door. The son finally blurted out, "Dad, can you believe it? The *Free Press* even comes printed on paper." This young man is intelligent in school, but his cultural experiences didn't include printed newspapers.

As a recent University of Georgia football game was being televised, my wife and I watched on the student section to catch a glimpse of our granddaughter who was on the "Spike Squad"—which is a pretty big deal at UGA. In the midst of the game, the TV camera panned the student section, and nearly all of them had their attention directed to their smartphones instead of the game on the field. I have noticed that at major college and professional football venues, many people watch the game on the matrix board or on the televisions in their suites instead of watching the field. Pay attention as you walk through a mall or are sitting in a restaurant, and count the number of people who are *not* looking at their phones. This may explain why some people are more comfortable watching the video screen in worship services rather than looking in a hymnal. Today's emphasis on visual stimulation (electronics over print) and on interactive experiences (social media) may lead people with extensive traditional experiences in church to feel disconnected as the church responds to digital cultural influences.

I hope it has become evident that worship services in most churches today are almost always exercises in cross-cultural communication. In the past, the term *cross-cultural* referred to blending racial and ethnic categories—and that is still an important area of emphasis. Now, it also applies to people who are accustomed to living in different eras of social change. Thus, a local congregation's methods of operation will likely be unfamiliar (and possibly uncomfortable) to someone in the congregation at any given point in time—either to those rooted in traditional experiences or to those seeking innovative experiences. The lack of familiarity with procedures in a worship service can lead people to feel out of place, and that creates a tendency to tune out what is happening. Those kinds of responses work against the purposes of worship. It is important to explain the purposes of our methodologies in the church. This will educate newcomers and reinforce the importance of those practices for believers who may have forgotten that.

As we transition from looking at cultural disconnections in the methods of the church to cultural disconnections in the message of the church, I want to shift focus for a short time from the Body of Christ as a whole to ministers, teachers, and other church leaders. In many local congregations, the methodology used in church programs is determined by one or more people in a leadership position. Several important questions need to be considered:

- How does a tradition-influenced minister lead people who do not have an extensive background in church activities, and who are accustomed to living in a world of rapid cultural change?
- How does a minister whose life has been lived largely in the ongoing present tense effectively lead people who are cognitively and emotionally tied to traditional church programs?
- How does ongoing acceleration of social change impact the relationship between the ministerial staff and selected church leaders when cultural disconnect occurs?

The existence of cultural disconnect between church leaders and church members who have a wide range of cultural experiences has to be bridged so that a unified Body of Christ can be what God designed it to be.

When I took an evangelism course in a Bible college many years ago, the Professor said, "What you win people with is what you win people to." We were told that evangelistic efforts had to be based on "winning people to Jesus by sharing the gospel message with them." I have noticed that quote in print a number of times through the years. One of the latest instances was in the book *Ministry Mantra: Language for Cultivating Kingdom* by J.R. Briggs and Bob Hyatt. Mr. Hyatt eloquently made the case for biblical worship at a time when culturally influenced methods are becoming more evident. Here is one of his powerful observations in the form of a question: "Is the reality of the presence of Christ among a people of love, inviting us to worship together as we gather around His table, no longer enough?" The programs developed in a local congregation must be centered on the gospel as revealed in Scripture. It is the power of the Holy Spirit and not current cultural influences that lead people to Christ and helps them grow in their spiritual lives. Paying attention to the cultural experiences of church attenders enables the gospel to be packaged in ways that communicate with diverse groups of people. The substance of our methods must be the gospel, even if various forms are used.

VIII

CULTURAL DISCONNECT IN PROCLAIMING THE MESSAGE OF THE CHURCH

ANOTHER AREA WHERE SOCIAL change in the church has created disconnect involves the way we talk about our faith. If I were to say to you, *"En arshee een o logos kai o logos een pros tone theeon, kai o theeos een o logos,"* would that mean anything to you? Those transliterated Greek words are found in **John 1:1**, and are translated as, *"In the beginning was the Word and the Word was with God and the Word was God."* In today's world, many people react to traditional religious terms like you probably reacted to my presentation of the Greek words. Without experience in studying the Greek language, those words have little meaning for you.

Jonathan Merritt (*Learning to Speak God from Scratch*) suggests that some people who are only marginally involved in church activities accuse Christians of speaking "Christianese," and that is a language they don't understand. Understanding Christian words and ideas is best accomplished through the study of Scripture where we can find objective reference points to define and explain those words and ideas. The problem with "Christianese" is that many of those terms were coined by religious leaders through the years, and are not found in Scripture. Therefore, there is no objective source to discover their meanings. Terms like *rapture, original sin, eternal security, communion,* and *altar call* may have validity in religious rhetoric, but they may not be understood by people without traditional religious experiences. There is nothing wrong with using these words, but we do need to remember that they have real meaning only to people who have been exposed to those expressions. We are on safer ground in cross-cultural communication when we use Bible words for Bible things. And, we need to remember to explain those sacred words fully when we do use them. Words like *justification* and *sanctification* (just to name two) need to be fully explained when used if all believers are to be *edified* (another word to be explained). Some of our religious tracts and some evangelistic programs are filled with words that probably have little or no meaning to a nonbeliever in today's culture, because those people do not have traditional church experiences.

More than a century ago, sociologist William Graham Sumner in *Folkways* (1911) wrote about this issue. He wrote about culture in general, but his writing can be applied specifically to church life: "[C]ommunal habits and customs (like the use of Christianese), over time, form an in-group and develop favoritism for the insiders to the exclusion of the outsiders." This pioneer in the field of sociology wrote this after looking back on human history, and the observations are still valid. The communal habits and customs may look different in the twenty-first century, but in-groups still develop in our local congregations. When in-groups develop, then out-groups will result and interpersonal disconnections will occur.

Our religious words can become our passwords and secret handshakes—our "shibboleths."

Shibboleths are defined as customs, traditions, or speech patterns that distinguish the in-group from outsiders. This word is found in the Bible in **Judges 12:5–6 [NLT]**.

> **Jephthah captured the shallow crossings of the Jordan River, and whenever a fugitive from Ephraim tried to go back across, the men of Gilead would challenge him. "Are you a member of the tribe of Ephraim?" they would ask. If the man said, "No, I'm not." They would tell him to say "SHIBBOLETH." If he was from Ephraim, he would say "Sibboleth" because people from Ephraim cannot pronounce that word correctly.**

We can identify "outsiders" (people from different cultural backgrounds) when they don't know our sacred words and or follow our procedures in church. And those who don't have that knowledge feel like they are outsiders. An investigation of religious writings, songs, and sermons will show us that there are several generations of Christianese and shibboleths used in our churches today. Each generation contributes to the compilation of religious language. Those who teach and preach need to be aware of their responsibility to communicate God's Word with clarity in order to bring unity of understanding to people with diverse cultural experiences. It is not prudent to assume that everyone in attendance is acquainted with the same words and ideas that we possess and use.

Sir Philip Gibbs wrote in his book *The Cross of Peace* (1935): "Modern progress has made the world a neighborhood; God has given us the task of making it a brotherhood." Little did Sir Philip know in 1935 just how great a task lies before the Body of Christ in the twenty-first century and beyond. While physical and social distances have been narrowed through innovations in communication and transportation, those innovations have also opened the door to a highly differentiated world neighborhood. Therefore, it is important to find ways to bring people with divergent cultural backgrounds into a harmonious, united fellowship of believers. Our sibling relationships within the Body of Christ must be recognized and valued. Creating and sustaining strong fellowship ties must be viewed as a mandate from God to build a unified church in all cultures and in every era.

Previously in this book, the process of communication was described as involving senders who encode messages that have meaning to them and transmitting that message to receivers who try to decode the message to find meaning for themselves. What was not mentioned was that all these transmissions occur within a social context. To this point, the discussion about cultural disconnect that occurs in proclaiming God's messages has focused on finding wording that gets the speaker and the listening on the same page. There are other issues besides language that affect spiritual communication in local congregations.

The Lewis Center for Church Leadership published an adaptation of Charley Reeb's book *That'll Preach!* In that article, Mr. Reeb advocated the one-point sermon, because listening is harder work than many people want to invest. Therefore, the task of the speaker is to keep listeners engaged in hearing God's Word.

When I took preaching classes (Homiletics), the professors all stressed the importance of a three-point sermon with lots of illustrations and an emotional closing. At that time, I believe we were told that the average attention span of adults in America was twenty-eight minutes—the length of the average sitcom on television. Recent data from several sources indicate that there are two kinds of attention spans to consider. The *transient attention span* that a person has when not focused on anything in particular is between nine and twelve seconds. The *selective attention span* that a person has when focused on a task or listening to something varies between ten and twenty minutes. That data also indicates that some people can refocus after being distracted, but that varies from person to person.

Neil Postman, in his book *Amusing Ourselves to Death*, suggests that there is an inverse relationship between attention spans and involvement with technology. He wrote that attention spans decrease as the amount of television viewing and Internet browsing increase. It is reasonable to assume that most local congregations are composed of people with a wide range of exposure to electronic and digital devices. Assuming that the writings of Charley Reeb and Neil Postman are correct, what are the implications for worship services and Sunday school classes in our local congregations? There is no reason to believe that people are going to lessen their exposure to digital communication. Therefore, there is a need for adaptations to occur in the way we present messages from God in our church programs.

I had a discussion recently with a pastor who had heard complaints from members of the congregation that his sermons were too lengthy. He told the people from the pulpit that if they could sit for three hours at a football game, they could listen to 45-minute sermons. When we met, I gave him an illustration. I asked him how much water could a five-gallon bucket hold. After giving me a funny look, he told me that, obviously, it would hold five gallons. Then I asked him how much water that bucket would hold if I ran water from the hose into the bucket for 45 minutes. He agreed that it would only hold five gallons. I remarked that there was value in considering the receptivity of listeners. Only time will tell if my illustration had influence on the pastor.

When I directed a statewide association that regulates high school athletics, I was asked quite often to do interviews with the media. Being a verbose person by nature, I gave interviews to print media that were wordy. As I did more television interviews, I learned to speak in sound bites rather than sentences and paragraphs. People who watch TV news or who browse Internet news frequently begin to think in sound bites. Some of you are old enough to remember regular correspondence that was done through multipage letters. Now, think about communication through messaging technology that has these limits:

- Instant messaging—160 characters
- Twitter—280 characters (up from 140)
- Instagram messaging—1,000 characters

The exposition of Scripture really can't be reduced to the level of electronic communication, but preachers and teachers need to make some accommodations to the experience levels of those listeners who regularly utilize modern technology.

Another kind of disconnect is only partially influenced by culture. That issue involves the diverse spiritual maturity of attendees in services at our local congregations. When a pastor or a teacher speaks to an assembly on Sunday, the audience will likely include people who have not accepted Christ as Savior and Lord, people who are spiritual infants, people who are spiritually mature, and people who are somewhere in between. How does God's message get communicated to such a diverse audience that has limited attention spans and a desire for instant messaging?

There is no question that the Holy Spirit works in the hearts and minds of people despite the cultural disconnect that has been mentioned. I wonder how much more could be accomplished for God's Kingdom, if we could find ways to become better connected to God and to one another. A friend of mine told me of a dream he had in which Jesus showed him an elaborate pencil drawing on a mural. Jesus explained that was my friend's life and showed him various situations he had experienced. Then Jesus took him to another room and there was a mural in vivid color and it was more elaborate than the previous mural. Then Jesus told him that this was the way his life could be if he had committed himself more fully to resources that Jesus provides. That dream is an illustration about the way we proclaim God's message in today's world. We can transform life in a local congregation from the pencil drawing of our disconnected fellowship to a vividly colorful depiction of God's plans to unite believers in a culturally disconnected world. We need to remember that the Holy Spirit is not chained to the patterns of any particular culture or to personal preferences that a group of believers might have.

IX

PRINCIPLES FOR UNITING A CHANGING CHURCH

BUILDING UNITY IN THE contemporary church is a difficult task that requires God's guidance and power. It also requires a willingness of members of the Body of Christ to love Jesus more than they love the cultural trappings (past or present) that influence their lives. I believe that the ideas that have been put forth in this book can lead us to formulate some principles for building unity in the midst of cultural change, cultural acceleration, and cultural disconnect. These eleven principles do not form a complete list for applying "God's Gorilla Glue" to restore and sustain unity in the contemporary church. I anticipate that readers can add to this list based on their experiences in the church.

1. We need to recognize that unity can and should exist in the midst of diversity and social change. Carl Ketcherside (*The Twisted Scriptures*) correctly pointed out, "We are brothers (and sisters) because we have the same Father; not because we have the same opinions." It is difficult to program unity, but continual Bible-centered preaching and teaching stressing

that we have been adopted into God's family (reconciled to Him) through Christ's sacrifice on the cross. All those who are members of God's family are spiritual siblings to one another regardless of their cultural differences.

2. We need to remind ourselves that the work of the Holy Spirit in our local congregations is not restricted just to traditional views or to new approaches alone. The essential goals, expectations, and roles for the Body of Christ are specified in the New Testament, and they should be followed. Church activities that are not specified in the Bible (and are not contrary to Scripture) may be acceptable, but they are always matters of opinion and preference. Therefore, those activities can be subject to change without harming the mission of the Body of Christ.

3. We need to recognize that effective evangelism will usually bring people into our local congregations from a wide range of cultural experiences. Those being added to the Body of Christ probably will not have a large collection of traditional church experiences. They won't be familiar with our religious terminology, and they may not be familiar (or comfortable) with our traditional programing. The joy of adding new members to the Body of Christ needs to be more important to us than avoiding any discomfort we experience with cross-cultural interactions.

4. It is important for Christians to understand that a Bible-based congregation can sustain its mission even when there are changes in its methods or organizational structure. Opportunities for the spiritual growth of church members must be available to people from all eras of social change—using methods with which they are familiar. Spiritual growth always involves change as we move on from where we used to be spiritually. That growth may be uncomfortable (or even

painful) at times, but the results are well worth the effort. We need to understand that the spiritual maturity that is realized through spiritual growth administered by the Holy Spirit is what helps Christians work through rapid social change in an effective way.

5. We need to have voices of reason in our local congregations today that can unify people from different cultural backgrounds into a united fellowship. Unity does not occur on the first meeting of people with different cultural experiences. It takes time to develop. We begin by relating to other people as individuals and not as members of some cultural category. Unity will only occur when people listen to one another in an attempt to understand where they have come from culturally and spiritually. The apostle Paul dealt with that very issue as Jews and Gentiles were coming to Christ. We can find a model for building unity in Paul's approach to ministry as recorded in **I Corinthians 9:22b–23 [NLT]**.

> *I try to find common ground with everyone, doing everything I can to save some. I do everything to spread the Good News and share its blessings.*

Our commonality is found in Christ (the head of the church), and that commonality is more important than any differences we might have. Once again Carl Ketcherside has great words of wisdom for us (*The Twisted Scriptures*) when he wrote: "Unity in Christ is not conformity, but community. We are one because we share a common faith and not because we hold the same opinions."

6. We need to understand that our personal preferences about church activities do not create a mandate for other people to follow, but our preferences shouldn't be ignored either. When you feel threatened by cultural change, focus on what you can

control—i.e., your responsibilities to be a productive member of the Body of Christ. Those responsibilities are to be carried out regardless of your emotional responses to how much you like or dislike the programs of the local congregation.

Situations such as the speed of change in life, by themselves, do not determine our feelings. Our emotional reactions are based on how we define and interpret those situations. Change will not be a threat unless we define it as a threat. We need to understand and respect the preferences of those from other races, ethnicities, gender, or eras of social change. Respect for the preferences of others is a concept Paul taught in **Romans 12:-9-10 [NASV]**:

> *Love must be free of hypocrisy. Detest what is evil, cling to what is good.*
> *Be devoted to one another in brotherly love; give preference to one another in honor.*

Hypocritical love occurs when we say we love God and Christ, but don't love one another (**I John 4:21**). When we have *agape* love for another person, we will want to honor their preferences even if those preferences aren't "our cup of tea." With a body of believers in the church, there should be reciprocal love so that other people are willing to honor our preferences on occasion. Paul revealed some guidelines that Christians can use to develop harmonious relationships in **Romans 12:16–18 [NLT]**.

> *Live in harmony with each other. Don't be too proud to enjoy the company of ordinary people. And don't think you know it all. Never pay back evil with more evil. Do things in such a way that everyone can see that you*

are honorable. Do all that you can to live in peace with everyone.

Throughout the New Testament, the phrase *same mind* is used to refer to people who obey God's commands, and who make the "mind of Christ" their model for viewing other people. "Having the same mind" does not mean that all Christians have to agree on every issue that is not covered with a biblical prescription. And, when we have different opinions about the way the local congregation operates, we are to interact with others humbly, respectfully, and peacefully.

Alexander Campbell used a motto that had been used by Christian leaders for many years in Europe when he said, "In essentials unity; in opinions liberty; in all things love."

He was approached by a man who said that there would be no unity in the church because everyone had opinions. Campbell responded by saying, "We do not ask people to give up their opinions—we ask them not to impose them on others" (Sermonindex.net—"Quotes of Alexander Campbell").

7. As has been stated in previous principles, unity in the Body of Christ in a cross-cultural setting means that Christians will have to give in to the preferences of others on occasion. Failure to do this results in disconnect among believers who are experiencing "cultural egocentrism." People living with that view believe the world should revolve around their preferences. Paul addressed that concept when he wrote to the Christians in Ephesus in **Ephesians 5:20–21 [NLT]**.

And give thanks for everything to God the Father in the name of our Lord Jesus Christ. And further, submit to one another out of reverence for Christ."

The Greek word translated as *submit* was a military term that described what happened when a young man enlisted under the leadership of a particular general to join the army. In addition to the definition of the word, the Greek grammar has an important message for us. In the English language, there are two voices for verbs—active and passive. An example of an active voice verb is seen in this sentence: "John hit the ball." An example of a passive voice verb is seen in this sentence: "John was hit by the ball." In the active voice, the subject (*John*) acted on the object (*ball*). In the passive voice, the subject (*John*) was acted upon by the object (*ball*). That is quite a difference in meaning. In Greek grammar, there is also a middle voice wherein the subject does something to or for the self. Paul's concept of submission to other people in the middle voice indicates this is a voluntary act where we (the subject) do something to or for ourselves. We give ourselves permission to let others have their preferences, and they will do the same for us in a unified fellowship. We are willing to do this to benefit the cause of Christ and the advancement of God's Kingdom.

8. Christians are able to mend many fractures in the Body of Christ when we remember how to speak to each other properly. Well-chosen words empower us to express compassion and extend kindness to other people—especially when we are in the midst of cultural disconnect. Paul stressed the importance of Christians talking properly to one another in **Ephesians 4:29 [NASV]:**

> *Let no unwholesome word proceed from your mouth, but only such a word as is good for edification according to the need of the moment, that it may give grace to those who hear.*

PRINCIPLES FOR UNITING A CHANGING CHURCH | 111

This passage indicates there are several desired outcomes that result from proper talk: We are to build up people (*edify*) and we are to provide the grace that others need at that particular time. Speech that accomplishes such results according to Paul is "wholesome." The root of the English word *wholesome* is *whole*. In mathematics, there are whole numbers and fractions. Unwholesome words fractionalize people—make them less than they are. Using proper words enables Christians to bring out the best in others (and ourselves), and that makes the Body of Christ stronger. When Christians exhibit the mind of Christ, they speak properly to others, and those words contain spiritually revitalizing messages. When we are given the task of transmitting such valuable messages, we need to be certain that we are handling them with a Christlike spirit.

9. We need to understand that solidarity is not necessarily the same thing as unity. People can bond together against a common enemy for self-serving reasons—not for the good of the entire group. Some people may remember old Western movies in which pioneers in a wagon train circled their wagons when attacked. That didn't mean those people got along with each other before or after the attack, but they were willing to work together in a crisis. A modern example of apparent solidarity that may not be producing unity is seen in the rise of political activism among conservative, evangelical religious groups. We live in an in-your-face society as demonstrated in sports, television programs, movies, and politics. The common modus operandi in these areas involves looking for enemies, then confronting and fighting them. The impersonal nature of social media that accompanies in-your-face attitudes affords people an opportunity to say things they wouldn't normally say face-to-face. Unfortunately, Christians are not immune to this worldly behavior, and it hurts church unity and

the church's testimony to the world. Speaking out together against ungodly values in our culture does not guarantee that there is unity in the Body of Christ. Christians do need to speak out against the rampant immorality in our world, but Paul's admonition to **"Speak the truth in love"** (**Ephesians 4:15**) needs to be followed. Just recognizing and resisting outside enemies does not fulfill the mission of the Body of Christ in our disconnected world. When the church needs to circle the wagons in times of crisis, we must be certain that we are interested in advancing God's Kingdom and not just protecting the cultural interests with which we feel most comfortable. We must be certain we are carrying out God's plan for the Body of Christ in this era of cultural disconnect under the headship of Christ.

10. We need to understand that culture is something people learn. It is not wired into us at birth. Therefore, people can learn to change cultural opinions and preferences that disconnect them from other people. The indwelling Holy Spirit does provide wiring for Christians on the things that we should never change—the eternal truths that God has revealed in His Word. In the midst of challenging times culturally, Christians have reason to be optimistic, because God is still at work in us!
11. 11. We need to understand the overriding truth found in **Hebrews 13:8 [NASV]**:

Jesus Christ is the same yesterday, and today, yes, and forever.

This does not mean that Jesus is stuck in a particular cultural framework and never changes. It means that God and Christ operate above the structures of human cultures, and they accomplish magnificent things in all cultures and in all generations. That is really good news for the Body of Christ!

We can live as effective members of the Body of Christ regardless of how many cultural influences try to divide us. We must make certain that we keep growing spiritually to be more like Christ, and that we accept the reality that the Body of Christ includes other followers of Christ who are not exactly like us.

www.ingramcontent.com/pod-product-compliance
Lightning Source LLC
Chambersburg PA
CBHW071731090426
42738CB00011B/2455